CHARLIE CHAPLIN

CHARLIE
THE BEAUTY OF SILENCE
CHAPLIN

ALAN SCHROEDER

An Impact Biography
FRANKLIN WATTS
A Division of Grolier Publishing
New York London Hong Kong Sydney
Danbury, Connecticut

Title Page:*The Little Tramp frolics with wood nymphs in* Sunnyside *(1919).*

Photographs ©: AP/Wide World Photos: 40, 55; Archive Photos: 42 (Popperfo-
to); Brown Brothers: 3, 13, 51; Corbis-Bettmann: 62 (Springer), 70, 73, 138,
139; Culver Pictures: 19, 25, 49; Photofest: 83, 101, 103, 108, 115, 123, 129;
UPI/Corbis-Bettmann: 64, 67, 86, 97, 137.

Library of Congress Cataloging-in-Publication Data

Schroeder, Alan
    Charlie Chaplin : the beauty of silence / Alan Schroeder
      p. cm. – (An Impact biography)
    Includes bibliographical information and index.
    ISBN 0-531-11317-5 (lib. bdg.)   ISBN 0-531-15864-0 (pbk.)
    1. Chaplin, Charlie, 1889–1977–Juvenile literature. 2. Motion picture
    actors and actresses–United States–Biography–Juvenile literature.
    3. Comedians–United States–Biography–Juvenile literature. I. Title
    PN2287.C5S36 1997
    791.43'028'092–dc20
    [B]   96-30334
                                                                   CIP
                                                                   AC

To Alice Gomach and Giselle Reisman, with love

CONTENTS

CHARLIE CHAPLIN

1
"FELLER'S PRETTY FUNNY"

IN THE FALL OF 1912, film director Mack Sennett spent six days traveling by train from Los Angeles to New York City. He was accompanied by his twenty-year-old girlfriend and leading lady, Mabel Normand. According to Sennett, he told Normand he had some important business to take care of in New York, after which they could "do the town, see all the shows, and have a big fling in the fine restaurants."

One of the productions they saw while in New York was *A Night in an English Music Hall,* featuring a gifted comedian named Charlie Chaplin. Like most directors, Sennett was always looking for new talent, and throughout the act he kept noticing Chaplin's antics. Playing a middle-aged drunk, Chaplin, too, was "watching" the show from a box seat. At one point, said Sennett, the drunk tumbled from his box onto the stage "and took part in a knockabout comic fight with the other English actors. . . .

"'Feller's pretty funny,' Mabel said.

"'Think he'd be good for pictures?' [Sennett] said.

"'He might be.'"[1]

11

Sennett made a note to keep Chaplin in mind, but six months were to pass before he thought of the English comic again. By then, the director was back at his studio in Edendale, California, where he was having trouble with Ford Sterling, his leading male comic. Sterling was threatening to quit, and if he did, Sennett knew he would have to find a replacement in a hurry. He therefore contacted his partners in New York, asking them to locate Chaplin and invite him to come to California to appear in some one- and two-reel comedies (a reel typically ran thirteen minutes in length).

Chaplin, a cautious man, was not sure how to respond. It had taken him years to build a name for himself in the business, and he hesitated to quit vaudeville for what he called the "canned drama" of motion pictures. But in the end, he decided to give it a try. The money was good, and besides, if he hated the "flickers," he could always return to the stage.

In this hopeful frame of mind, Chaplin arrived in Los Angeles in early December 1913. After renting a small hotel room, he decided to attend the evening show at the Empress Theater. As it happened, Mack Sennett and Mabel Normand were also at the Empress that evening. They were sitting just two rows behind Chaplin, and after the show they invited the comedian to join them for supper at a nearby restaurant. Chaplin felt extremely nervous meeting his new boss and, according to Sennett, their conversation was stilted. Chaplin could tell by the look on Sennett's face that something was wrong.

"I thought you were a much older man," the director finally admitted.

Having only seen Chaplin once before, in full make-up, Sennett had guessed his age at about forty-five. But the comic, he now realized, was much younger, closer to twenty. Chaplin, who had heard this complaint before, was quick to respond. "I can make up as old as you like," he assured Sennett. Nevertheless, the thirty-three-year-old director had his doubts.

*Producer and director Mack Sennett ran Keystone, the leading
movie studio in the slapstick comedy field.*

A Canadian by birth, Sennett knew every angle of the movie business. For years, he had worked under legendary director D. W. Griffith at Biograph, one of the earliest motion picture studios. Then, in the summer of 1912, Sennett had teamed up with two partners to form a new company, Keystone, which specialized in slapstick comedy. According to Sennett, he and his "team of professional slam-bangers" were soon turning out some of the funniest one-reelers in the business. "We made a million dollars so fast," he said, "my fingers ached from trying to count."[2]

By the time Chaplin joined Keystone in late 1913, Sennett had proved himself one of the industry's most profitable directors. Among his moneymaking inspirations were the hilariously inept Keystone Kops and the lovely parade of women known as Mack Sennett's Bathing Beauties. He was also responsible for launching the short, but fabulous, career of Roscoe "Fatty" Arbuckle, one of the most popular comedians of the silent era. Other talented performers on Sennett's payroll included Mabel Normand, Fred Mace, Ford Sterling, Hank Mann, Minta Durfee, Chester Conklin, Mack Swain, and Alice Davenport.

In theory, Chaplin could not have selected a better training ground than Keystone to begin his career as a motion picture comedian. Unfortunately, his first few months with Mack Sennett were extremely frustrating.

Soon after meeting his new boss, Chaplin made his way to the Keystone Studio in Edendale, a short distance from Los Angeles. Stepping off the streetcar, his first view of the twenty-eight-acre lot was not encouraging. To the untrained eye, Keystone appeared to be nothing more than a collection of sagging barns and bungalows, surrounded by a green board fence. For a while, Chaplin stood across the road, looking uneasily at the main gate. Then, suffering a sudden attack of shyness, he returned to his hotel.

The same thing happened the following day, and the day after that. Finally, Sennett telephoned Chaplin, demanding to know why he had not shown up for work.

Sennett's impatience gave the comedian the courage he needed to pass through the studio gate.

Two years later, a newspaper reporter named Rose Wilder Lane wrote a book about Chaplin's early film career. In *Charlie Chaplin's Own Story*, Lane brought alive the busy, bewildering atmosphere of the Keystone Studio as Chaplin must have experienced it. "Hundreds of actors," she wrote, "were strolling about in costume; carpenters were hammering away at new sets; five companies were playing before five clicking cameras. There was a roar of confused sound—screams, laughs, an explosion, shouted commands, pounding, whistling, the bark of a dog. The air was thick with the smell of new lumber in the sun, flashlight powder, cigarette smoke."[3]

Chaplin spent his first weeks at Keystone exploring the lot, waiting for Sennett to put him to work. Occasionally, he said, he would meet the director in passing, "but he would look through me, preoccupied. I had an uncomfortable feeling that he thought he had made a mistake in engaging me."[4]

After a month of inactivity, Chaplin was finally assigned his first film, a one-reeler called *Making a Living*. Mabel Normand was supposed to be his costar, but after watching Chaplin rehearse, she decided to bow out. The "little Englisher," she confided to Sennett, had been much funnier in New York.

Making a Living was shot in three days, a typical length of time for a Keystone production. It was directed by Henry "Pathé" Lehrman and, from the start, there was trouble on the set. Chaplin found the steady clicking of the camera unnerving and, to everyone's annoyance, he seemed unable to stay within the camera's limited range. Wasted film began to pile up at an alarming rate. Aggravating the situation, Chaplin kept making artistic suggestions to Lehrman, who resented the interference. Their relationship became so antagonistic that Sennett was forced to intervene.

Making a Living was supposed to launch Chaplin as a bright new talent, but when Sennett saw the finished film, he considered it worthless. So did Chaplin, who made up his mind to quit the movie business as soon as possible. "I'll never catch on," he told comedian Chester Conklin. "It's too fast. I can't tell what I'm doing, or what anybody wants me to do." Conklin, also a newcomer to Keystone, advised him to stick it out: "I told him he was going to be . . . very big in motion pictures. I lied like hell. I didn't think any such thing."

Sennett, by this time, had started work on a new picture, *Mabel's Strange Predicament.* One day, during a rainstorm, he realized he was stuck for an idea. Turning to Chaplin, he told him to put on a costume: "Anything will do." Racking his brain for an idea, Chaplin retreated to the men's dressing room, which he shared with Ford Sterling, Chester Conklin, and Fatty Arbuckle. The three actors were playing cards, waiting for the rain to let up.

Glancing around the dressing room, Chaplin noticed Arbuckle's trousers hanging on a chair. He put them on. The huge pants looked ridiculous on his slight frame and the comics started to laugh. Next, Chaplin selected a tight overcoat and a small derby. Then he picked up a thin bamboo cane and began to perform tricks with it. "The cane seemed to come alive in his hand," said Conklin. "It *gestured.* He tipped his hat with it. His starched cuff came loose, slid down the cane, and shot back to his wrist."[5]

Next, Chaplin spotted a pair of men's shoes, size fourteen. They were so large that, to keep them from falling off, he had to wear each shoe on the wrong foot. As a final touch, he borrowed a fake mustache and trimmed it to toothbrush size. This, he knew, would make him look older. Then, stepping back, Chaplin studied himself in the mirror.

Everything about the costume was a contradiction— the baggy pants, the tight coat, the small derby, the big shoes. Nothing fit properly, and that made the costume funny. "I had no idea of the character," Chaplin admitted.

"But the moment I was dressed, the clothes and the make-up made me feel the person he was."[6]

Years later, Chaplin would claim that the character of the Little Tramp was "fully born" by the time he returned to the set. The Keystone films reveal, however, that this was not the case. In 1914, when he first appeared on the screen, the Little Tramp was a vulgar and often mean-spirited character (one writer called his behavior "cruel, sometimes to the point of sadism"). In fact, more than a year would pass before the Tramp would begin to take on a more sympathetic personality. And yet, in one respect, Chaplin's memory was accurate: the basic costume and makeup seem to have come together almost instantly, as though the comedian's entire career had been leading up to this moment.

Hurrying back to the set, Chaplin "introduced" the Little Tramp to Sennett, who laughed at the absurdity of the costume. Then, to the director's amusement, Chaplin began to stroll around the stage, inventing little gags on the spot. As he had done in the dressing room, he used his cane imaginatively. He twirled it in the air; caught it on a coatrack; used it to pull up the back of his sagging trousers. Taking a swig from an imaginary bottle, he staggered about, pretending to be drunk. "He got his foot caught in the cuspidor," remembered Conklin. "[His] mustache wiggled like a rabbit's nose. A crowd gathered."

As much as Sennett enjoyed Chaplin's joking, he could not use the character of the Little Tramp in *Mabel's Strange Predicament*.[7] Instead, he assigned Chaplin to another film that was about to go into production, *Kid Auto Races at Venice*. To avoid the trouble of building a set, many Keystone comedies were shot outdoors, often at a public event. *Kid Auto Races*, for instance, was to be filmed at a children's soapbox derby not far from Los Angeles. "We had no story," said Sennett. "We merely cherished the hope . . . that if we turned [Chaplin] loose to get in the way of newsreel cameras and racing automobiles, [we] might be able to photograph something funny."[8]

Chaplin was frustrated to learn that once again he would be working with Pathé Lehrman, whom he regarded as a mediocre director. This time, however, there were fewer problems on the set. For one thing, *Kid Auto Races* was a relatively easy film to produce—the whole thing was shot in the space of a few hours. And to Chaplin's surprise, Lehrman not only listened to his suggestions, but actually used one of them to set the plot into motion.

In *Kid Auto Races*, Lehrman plays an irritable director trying to film a soapbox derby; Chaplin, as the Tramp, is fascinated by the hand-cranked camera and keeps trying to get into the picture. The five-minute comedy appealed to audiences and critics alike. "*Kid Auto Races*," said one trade journal, "[strikes] us as about the funniest film we have seen. . . . [Chaplin] does things we have never seen done on the screen before." After a rocky and unpromising start, Chaplin had discovered the screen character he was born to play.

In his book *Comedy Films,* John Montgomery suggests one of the main reasons for Chaplin's instant success: "The tramp who emerged from the slap-happy studio at Edendale was not an Englishman or an American. His theme was universal, . . . as readily understood in Cairo or Tokyo as in Boston or Maine. Fundamentally, the peoples of the world are very much alike. And Chaplin knew this, because he was and is at heart an international clown."[9]

By the end of 1914, Charlie Chaplin had become one of the screen's most recognizable faces. He knew his worth, and when it came time to renew his contract, he asked for $1,000 per week. Sennett refused, claiming that not even *he* made that much money. "I know it," Chaplin replied, "but the public doesn't line up outside the box office when your name appears as they do for mine."

The two men were unable to come to terms, and after giving it a great deal of thought, Chaplin decided to leave Keystone. Sennett warned him that his popularity might soon fade, but as it turned out, Chaplin's love affair with the public was just beginning. Within a month, he signed on with another studio at $1,250 per week; a year later, in 1916, Chaplin's salary jumped to $10,000 per week. By then, he was writing and directing some of the funniest and most successful comedies in Hollywood history. Thanks to the medium of film, said one writer, Chaplin "has made more people laugh than any other man who ever lived. . . . [He is] the unquestioned King of Comedy."

In 1954, when Mack Sennett wrote his autobiography, he spoke fondly of his days with Chaplin at the Keystone Studio. Though he had been slow to recognize Chaplin's gifts, he did not hesitate now to praise his work and to pay

This 1915 photo shows the Keystone lot in Edendale, California. In 1913, Mack Sennett persuaded Charlie Chaplin to appear in his studio's comedies.

tribute to his genius as an actor and director. Nor did Sennett minimize the importance of the Little Tramp, the most popular—and perhaps the most enduring—character of the silent film era.

"I wonder," he wrote, "if in all the history of the world, giving the kings and captains and heroes and celebrated women their full due—I wonder if there was ever a single person so beloved and so well known . . . as that baggy-pants tramp invented by accident one rainy day in Edendale.

"As for Charles Spencer Chaplin, I am not at all sure that we know him."[10]

2
"A PITILESS TIME!"

CHARLIE CHAPLIN WAS BORN into a show business family. His mother, Hannah Hill, was a music-hall performer who went by the stage name of Lily Harley. An attractive woman with violet-blue eyes and long brown hair, Hannah was noted for her ability to imitate well-known actresses of the day.

Charlie's father, Charles Chaplin, Sr., was also an entertainer. The son of a butcher, he probably met Hannah in a London boardinghouse where the two were living in the spring of 1885. Hannah, who was unmarried, had just given birth to her first child, Sydney (the identity of Sydney's father remains uncertain). After a brief period of courtship, Charles and Hannah were married on June 22, 1885, three months after Sydney's birth.

The following year, Hannah began to appear on London stages, where she advertised herself as "That Charming Little Chanter, Lily Harley." Though she had a fine figure and a pleasing voice, Hannah never became a music-hall celebrity—almost always, her name appeared at the bottom of the bill. On the evening of April 16, 1889, she gave birth to her second son, Charles Spencer Chaplin, Jr. After that, she retired from the stage to devote herself to the duties of motherhood.

Her husband, on the other hand, enjoyed theatrical success early on. Possessed of a fine baritone voice, Charles Chaplin had the good fortune to introduce several popular songs on the stage. In time, he became a headliner, earning as much as forty pounds per week in London. In 1890, one year after his son's birth, he sailed to the United States, where he performed with success at the Union Square Theatre in New York City.

Unfortunately, the Chaplins' marriage was short-lived. At that time, most English music halls served alcohol, and between numbers the artists were expected to socialize at the bar with the customers. Like many vaudevillians, Charles became a heavy drinker, and this led to a series of domestic fights that destroyed the Chaplins' home life. Upon Charles's return from New York in 1890, he and Hannah decided to separate. It would be several years before young Charlie would see his father again.

Left on her own, Hannah found occasional work as a wet nurse. For emotional support, she turned to the church, where she managed to earn a few extra shillings sewing dresses for members of the congregation. She also tried at this time to resurrect her stage career. Unfortunately, Hanna's singing voice had a tendency to break at unexpected moments, prompting the audience to jeer and catcall. One night, when this happened, the stage manager spotted young Charlie standing in the wings. The manager had often noticed Charlie's backstage antics and, taking the boy by the hand, he led him onstage, where he encouraged him to perform a number.

Five-year-old Charlie was happy to oblige. Accompanied by the orchestra, he began to sing a popular tune. The rowdy audience was taken by surprise and, halfway through the song, patrons began to throw money onto the stage. Charlie was so delighted he immediately stopped singing and squatted down, explaining to the crowd that as soon as he had retrieved all the money, he would continue the song. The audience, made up mostly of soldiers, rewarded him with a gale of laughter and a fresh shower of coins.

From then on, it was nearly impossible for Hannah to find work in the theater. In desperation, she began to pawn her belongings to feed and clothe her two sons. Sydney got a job selling newspapers, but his meager earnings were hardly enough to support a family of three. To survive, the Chaplins had to depend upon charity, standing in long lines to receive small parcels of food. "Victorian England," Charlie would later remark, "was a cruel, damnably cruel place. It was a pitiless time!"[1]

To lift the boys' spirits, Hannah would sometimes stage a show for them, performing her old music-hall numbers. On other occasions, she would sit at the window for hours, studying the passersby, trying to figure out who they were, where they were going, and why. She would share her humorous observations with Charlie, who delighted in this simple game.

"If it had not been for my mother," he said later, "I doubt if I could have made a success of pantomime. She was one of the greatest pantomime artists I have ever seen." By watching Hannah closely, he wrote, "I learned not only how to express my emotions with my hands and face, but also how to observe and study people."[2]

Shortly after Charlie's sixth birthday, Hannah fell ill. For some time, she had been suffering from migraine headaches, and in June 1895 she was admitted to the Lambeth Infirmary. Ten-year-old Sydney was placed temporarily in a school for the poor. Charlie, meanwhile, was sent to live with relatives of his mother's. According to a welfare report, both boys were eventually sent to a local workhouse "owing to the absence of their father and the destitution and illness of their mother."

Hannah remained hospitalized for four weeks. Upon her release, she was permitted a brief visit with her sons at the workhouse. Charlie was shocked by his mother's appearance; though Hannah was only thirty, she looked old and careworn. Together, she and the boys sat on a bench and wept over their common misfortune.

The following year, Sydney and Charlie were transferred to Hanwell, a charity school for orphans and destitute children. Here the brothers were separated: Sydney was sent to live with the older boys, while young Charlie was placed in the infants' ward. As he watched his brother being led away, Charlie felt frightened and bewildered. During his stay at the London workhouse, it had comforted him to think that his mother was nearby, "but at Hanwell," he said, "we seemed miles apart."

Charlie's life at the school was one of misery and loneliness. In general, he was a poor student, and his studies were an ongoing source of disappointment and trauma. In composition class, for instance, the teacher rapped Charlie's knuckles when he attempted to write with his left hand. To make matters worse, he came down with ringworm, a contagious skin disease. He was taken to the infirmary, where his head was shaved, smeared with iodine, then wrapped in a bandanna. "The treatment took weeks," he recalled, "and seemed like an eternity."

Every now and then, he would catch sight of his brother, who worked part-time in the kitchen. When Sydney could arrange it, he would smuggle bread rolls out to Charlie, who hid them under his jersey. The brothers had always been close, but it was here, at Hanwell, that their emotional bond was sealed for life.

Years later, Hannah's sister, Kate Mowbray, found it remarkable that anyone could "write about Charlie Chaplin without mentioning his brother Sydney. . . . Syd, of quiet manner, clever brain and steady nerve, has been father and mother to Charlie. Charlie always looked up to Syd, and Sydney would suffer anything to spare Charlie."[3]

Sydney Chaplin was very close to his half brother, Charlie. Sydney acted on the stage and in movies but devoted much of his life to handling Charlie's business affairs.

In the summer of 1898, the boys were transferred to Norwood, another charity institution. One day, Sydney was playing football with the other boys when he was called out of the game by two nurses. They informed him that his mother had lost her mind and had been taken to Cane Hill Lunatic Asylum. When Charlie heard the news, he felt a deep despair: "Why had she done this? Mother, so light-hearted and gay—how could she go insane?" Neither of the boys were aware that Hannah's condition may have been hereditary. A few years earlier, Hannah's own mother, Mary Ann Hill, had been committed to an insane asylum.

At this point, the court ordered Charles Chaplin, Sr., to assume custody of Sydney and Charlie. For nearly a decade, Charles had had little contact with his family, and he was not pleased to have this new responsibility thrust upon him. Nor was the situation acceptable to Louise, the woman with whom Charles was living. A bitter person, she took an instant dislike to Sydney and Charlie; more than once, in an angry fit, she locked them out of the house, forcing them to sleep in the street. She was relieved when, a few months later, the boys were returned to the care of their mother, who had been released from Cane Hill Asylum. To help support the family, Charles agreed to send his estranged wife ten shillings a week, a small amount but enough to put food on the table and coal in the stove.

Hannah and the boys managed to find cheap lodgings at 39 Methley Street, between a pickle factory and a slaughterhouse. The neighborhood was depressing, but Sydney and Charlie were happy to be back with their mother. To bring in money, Hannah rented a sewing machine and worked at home as a seamstress, assembling precut blouses for a sweatshop.

A traumatic episode from this period forever stood out in Charlie's memory. One afternoon, he saw a sheep being led to the slaughterhouse. Somehow, the animal escaped the butcher's grasp and began running down the street. A handful of children immediately took up the chase, trying to grab the sheep's tail. At first, Charlie was delighted by the slapstick scene—that is, until the wayward sheep was caught. At that moment, he realized that the struggling animal was going to be killed. He became hysterical and ran to his mother, screaming and weeping. Many years later, he wondered "if that episode did not establish the premise of my future films—the combination of the tragic and the comic."[4]

One day shortly thereafter, Hannah came across a humorous poem, "Miss Priscilla's Cat." She found it so delightful that she taught it to Charlie, who in turn recited it before his classmates. The teacher was so impressed by his reading that Charlie was given permission to recite "Miss Priscilla's Cat" before every class in the school. This experience, he later said, was extremely rewarding: "From having been an obscure and shy little boy I became the center of interest of both the teachers and the children. It even improved my studies."[5]

Somehow, word of Charlie's comedic talent reached the ears of his father. Charles Chaplin was so intrigued that he spoke to an acquaintance, William Jackson, who managed a dancing troupe known as the Eight Lancashire Lads. At the moment, Jackson was in need of an extra boy and agreed to hire Chaplin's son. Thus, at the age of nine, Charlie left school to become an entertainer.

The British music halls were then at their height, and the Eight Lancashire Lads were able to find steady work in London and the provinces. Though Charlie did not realize it at the time, the two years he spent with the Lads were invaluable to his future career as a comic. Week after week, he had the opportunity to observe at close range some of the leading comedians of the day—the Griffiths Brothers, for instance, who performed breathtaking stunts of lunacy on a trapeze. Charlie was especially fascinated by the clowns who mixed humor with moments of pathos, a sophisticated combination he would later perfect in his silent films.

While the Lads were touring the provinces, a new and exciting form of entertainment was sweeping the country. The first public showing of a motion picture had taken place in San Francisco in May 1880.[6] Audiences marveled at the sight of life-sized horses galloping across the screen, but fifteen years were to pass before the idea of moving pictures began to catch on. One of the earliest, and most celebrated, exhibitions took place in Paris in December 1895. Several months later, in the spring of 1896, motion pictures were shown at a popular music hall in New York City. A reporter from the *New York Times* was there to describe the event: "An unusually bright light fell upon the screen. Then came into view two precious blonde persons of the variety stage . . . doing the umbrella dance. . . . Their motions were all clearly defined."[7]

Soon, motion pictures were being shown in large cities throughout the world. Crudely photographed and jerky to watch, films of the late 1890s depicted simple, everyday events: *Demolition of a Wall, Sea Waves, Beavers at Play.* Because the black-and-white images were so new, and so unusual, people were unsure what to call them. For years, they were referred to variously as "living photographs," "shadow plays," "picture plays," "flickers," and "galloping tintypes." Inventor Thomas Edison called them "life-motion'd pictures," a phrase that never caught on.

Victorian audiences were fascinated—and sometimes bewildered—by what they saw on the screen. When *Sea Waves* was exhibited in New York, the people sitting in the first rows leapt back as the water approached the shore, fearful of getting splashed. For a few unforgettable moments, the line that separated reality from illusion had been blurred; according to one pair of historians, watching a movie in 1896 "was a new and godlike experience."

The projection of "living photographs" was one of the great scientific marvels of the nineteenth century. Yet the public's interest in them was surprisingly short-lived. As early as 1899, the novelty had worn off, and films like *Sea*

Waves were relegated to the back rooms of penny arcades. They were also shown as "chasers" in vaudeville houses—something to project on a sheet while the aisles were being cleared.

The movies might have faded away altogether had it not been for the release of *Cinderella* in 1900. Directed by a French magician, Georges Méliès, *Cinderella* was one of the first motion pictures to tell a story with a beginning, middle, and end. The fairy tale was divided into twenty tableaux, or scenes; the action of each tableau kept the plot moving forward. As obvious as this approach may sound, it nevertheless revolutionized the industry. More than a decade after the invention of the celluloid strip, film narrative had at last been discovered.

Méliès's *Cinderella* was an international success, and it's likely that the Eight Lancashire Lads saw the movie while they were touring. The French tale, in fact, was enjoying a healthy revival at the turn of the century. In addition to the Méliès film, there were several stage productions, one of which resulted in the Lads obtaining their most prestigious booking to date. In late 1900, they were invited to take part in a lavish Christmas pantomime, *Cinderella*, which opened on December 24 at the London Hippodrome. The Lads, who received no billing for their appearance, played domestic animals in a kitchen scene.

Charlie was dressed as a cat, and at the first children's matinee, he approached the rear end of a dog and began to sniff. The house manager, who was standing backstage, was horrified, but Charlie pretended not to notice. "After smelling the dog," he remembered, "I smelled the proscenium, then I lifted my leg. The audience roared—possibly because the gesture was uncatlike."[8] After the show, Charlie was roundly scolded by the manager, who told him that such vulgar behavior could close down the theater.

One night, the Eight Lancashire Lads performed at a charity benefit for Charlie's father, who had fallen upon hard times. Deeply moved by the generosity of his fellow artists, the once-popular singer made his way to the front of the stage, where he delivered a short speech. Watching from the wings, Charlie did not realize that his father was seriously ill. A few months later, in May 1901, Charles Chaplin died of cirrhosis of the liver, a disease associated with alcoholism. He was thirty-seven years old.

Hannah, meanwhile, had begun to fret about Charlie's health. He was too thin, she kept saying. Her motherly concern became so irritating to William Jackson that he finally sent Charlie home. Despite her son's tearful pleading, Hannah refused to let him return to the stage. According to Charlie, his mother's "most painful memories were of music hall life and she passionately made me promise never to act in one."[9]

During this period, Sydney accepted a job as a bugler aboard a passenger ship. He sent home what money he could, but Hannah and Charlie had barely enough to live upon. For the next two years, they moved from one squalid flat to another, finally occupying a cramped, third-floor garret at 3 Pownall Terrace. To earn money, Charlie sold flowers on the street, ran errands for a candlemaker, gave dancing lessons, and operated a printing press. He even tried his hand at glassblowing, but the heat from the furnace, he said, swiftly overcame him, "and I was carried out unconscious and laid on a sand pile."

Frustrated and discouraged, Charlie decided that, no matter what, he would return to the stage. One day, without telling his mother, he paid a visit to Blackmore's Theatrical Agency on Bedford Street. After Charlie's name and address had been entered in the register of actors, he was told politely by a clerk that if a boy's part became available, he would be called. Months passed, but Charlie heard nothing.

Hannah, meanwhile, was waiting impatiently for Sydney to return from sea. As the weeks slipped by, her personality began to change. Charlie noticed that his mother seemed listless and depressed; when the sewing machine was taken away for lack of payment, Hannah seemed unconcerned. One spring afternoon, Charlie returned to Pownall Terrace and heard from the neighborhood children that his mother had gone insane. Hurrying up the narrow flight of stairs, he found his mother sitting at the window, looking pale and tormented. Hannah's manner was so peculiar that Charlie burst into tears.

With the help of the landlady, he led his mother down the street to the nearest hospital. There, it was discovered that Hannah was suffering from malnutrition. The doctor who examined her reported that her behavior was "noisy and incoherent. . . . She says the floor is the river Jordan and she cannot cross it. At times violent and destructive."[10] When Charlie left the hospital that afternoon, he felt confused and heartbroken.

For days, he wandered the streets aimlessly, taking his meals where he could find them. He kept up his courage by telling himself again and again what a fine actor he was. "I had to feel that exuberance that comes from utter confidence in yourself," he explained. "Without that you go down to defeat."[11]

On May 11, 1903, Hannah was transferred again to Cane Hill Asylum. A week or so after that, Sydney returned from sea. He brought with him a crate of green bananas and enough money to live upon for the next few months. Sydney, too, had decided that he wanted to become an actor, but it was Charlie who achieved his dream first. One month after his brother's return, Charlie received a note asking him to come to Blackmore's Theatrical Agency. Wearing his best suit, he called upon Mr. Blackmore and, to his astonishment, was offered not one, but two acting jobs.

First, Blackmore told him, there was "an exceptionally good boy's part in a new play," *Jim, A Romance of Cockayne,* which was to have a trial engagement in Kingston. After that, Charlie was to play the role of Billy the page boy in a production of *Sherlock Holmes*, which would tour the provinces for forty weeks. For his services, he was offered two pounds ten shillings a week. Charlie could hardly believe what he was hearing.

Later, on the street, he felt a bit light-headed: "What had happened? It seemed the world had suddenly changed, had taken me into its fond embrace and adopted me. . . . I had suddenly left behind a life of poverty and was entering a long-desired dream—a dream my mother had often spoken about, had reveled in. I was to become an actor!"[12]

3

THE KARNO COMPANY

WHILE REHEARSING FOR *Jim, A Romance of Cockayne*, Charlie Chaplin began to learn the fundamentals of acting and stagecraft. The fourteen-year-old was taught how to make an entrance, how to deliver his lines, how to throw his voice so it could be heard in the balcony. At first, he recalled, "I moved my head and mugged too much when I talked," but this was soon corrected.

Jim opened at the Royal County Theatre in Kingston on July 6, 1903. Though the melodrama was panned by the press, Charlie's humorous performance as Sammy the newsboy was singled out for praise. "[Chaplin is] a bright and vigorous child actor," said one reviewer. "I have never heard of the boy before, but I hope to hear great things of him in the near future."[1]

A month later, on August 10, *Sherlock Holmes* began a long and successful tour of the provinces. The role of Billy the page boy was not large, but Charlie made it memorable, and once again he was praised by the critics for his "wonderfully clever acting." Three months into the run, he managed to get Sydney hired for one of the supporting roles, and for the next six months the Chaplin brothers toured together.

During this period, Hannah was released from Cane Hill Asylum, where she had spent the past eight months. She was feeling so well that she decided to join her sons on the road. For Charlie, it was a sentimental but painful reunion. Hannah, he said, seemed quiet, withdrawn, and strangely detached: "She acted more like a guest than our mother." A year later, Hannah once again lost her mind and was taken back to Cane Hill. This time, according to Charlie, the relapse was permanent.

While *Sherlock Holmes* was touring the provinces, Charlie and his brother must have noticed how popular—and how profitable—motion pictures were becoming. Nickelodeons, it seemed, were springing up everywhere. For a nickel, a patron could enter a darkened storefront, take a seat, and watch a half-hour program of films projected on a bedsheet. Usually, a pianist was on hand to provide musical accompaniment (contrary to their name, "silent" films were never watched in silence).

In the early 1900s, going to a nickelodeon was an exciting and affordable form of entertainment. Children were usually admitted two for a nickel, and Charlie probably saw a number of films while he was on tour. But as a "legitimate" stage performer, he wouldn't have dreamed of appearing in a movie himself. During this period, the "flickers" were dismissed by most actors as a crude form of amusement, unworthy of their talents. Even if Charlie had wanted to see his face projected on a bedsheet, it is unlikely he would have admitted it to anyone.

The *Sherlock Holmes* tour came to an end in June 1904. Financially, the production had been so successful that a second tour was arranged. All told, Charlie would spend a total of two and a half years touring the provinces in various productions of *Sherlock Holmes*, giving his final performance in March 1906.

Immediately thereafter, he joined another touring

company, *Casey's Court Circus*. The general director of the show, Will Murray, was highly impressed by Charlie's audition: "He sang, danced, and did a little of practically everything in the entertaining line. He had the makings of a 'star' in him, and I promptly took him on salary."[2]

In one of the funniest sketches in the show, Charlie had to run frantically around the stage, turning a series of sharp corners at top speed. According to Murray, it took "many weary hours" to perfect the maneuver. But the result was a visual treat. As Charlie approached each corner, he lifted one leg and began to hop on the other, nearly skidding to a stop. At the same time, one hand would fly to his hat, which heightened the sense of an abrupt halt. Then, turning sharply on his heel, Charlie would take off again in another direction. It was a breathtakingly funny sight, destined to be one of his liveliest screen trademarks.

Overall, Charlie thought *Casey's Court Circus* was a dreadful show; it nevertheless gave him an opportunity to develop his comedic and pantomimic skills. His brother, Sydney, meanwhile, had signed a contract with the Karno Company, one of England's best-known theatrical outfits. Sydney became so successful with this company that by the fall of 1906 he was touring the United States. On several occasions, he encouraged his boss, Fred Karno, to give Charlie an audition, but for some reason Karno kept putting him off.

Charlie stayed with *Casey's Court Circus* until July 1907. Shortly before leaving the troupe, he was given a chance to perform for a week without pay at Foresters' Music Hall in London. Because the theater was located in a Jewish neighborhood, Charlie decided to bill himself as "Sam Cohen, the Jewish Comedian." His performance, however, was a disaster and, to his horror, he was booed off the stage.

A discouraging period of unemployment followed. Charlie was now eighteen, an awkward age for the theater—too old for boys' parts, and a bit too young for leading roles. He had just about given up hope of ever returning to the stage when Fred Karno, called him in for an interview. Unfortunately, Karno's first impression was not favorable. He thought Charlie was too small and too shy "to do any good in the theatre, particularly in the knockabout comedies that were my specialty."

Years of experience had taught the impresario to trust his intuition. A former acrobat, Fred Karno knew instinctively how to make people laugh. He also had a flair for finding and developing talent. Yet when he met Charlie for the first time, he had serious doubts that the "pale, puny" teenager had much to contribute in the way of comedy. But something, perhaps his fondness for Sydney, prompted Karno to give the boy a chance. He asked Charlie if he thought he could play the villain in a piece called *The Football Match.* "All I need is the opportunity," Charlie assured him. He was rewarded with a two-week trial run.

The Football Match opened at the London Coliseum in February 1908. As Chaplin paced backstage, waiting to go on, he felt extremely nervous. That night, he recalled, "meant re-establishing my confidence and wiping out the disgrace of that nightmare at the Foresters'."[3]

He need not have worried. His performance that evening was a clever piece of pantomime that delighted everyone. The curtain rose to reveal an athletic training room. His back to the audience, Chaplin sauntered onstage alone, wearing an expensive coat, opera cape, and top hat—obviously a gentleman of distinction. Then, wheeling around, he turned to face the audience. His nose was bright red, indicating that he was a heavy drinker. The crowd began to laugh.

A moment later, Chaplin tripped over a dumbbell. Then, to everyone's amusement, he got his cane entangled in the straps of an upright punching bag, which smacked him in the face. This, naturally, set off a merry fight between himself and the bag. The fun really got underway when Chaplin realized that his pants were falling down, a sight that sent the crowd into hysterics.

The third night, Karno himself came to see the show. To his surprise, the audience burst into applause the moment Chaplin walked onstage. Karno was delighted by the antics that followed, and at the end of the two-week trial run, he called the teenager into his office to talk terms. That afternoon, Chaplin sent a triumphant telegram to his brother: "HAVE SIGNED CONTRACT FOR ONE YEAR AT FOUR POUNDS PER WEEK. LOVE, CHARLIE."

The Football Match played for fourteen weeks in London, then went on tour. Though Chaplin had plenty of personality in front of the footlights, no one knew what to make of him offstage. Because he could go for long periods without talking to anyone, his colleagues decided that he was unfriendly and snobbish. "[Chaplin] wasn't very likeable," admitted Karno. "Occasionally he would be quite chatty, but on the whole he was dour and unsociable. He lived like a monk, had a horror of drink, and put most of his salary in the bank as soon as he got it."[4]

A few months after joining the Karno Company, Chaplin fell in love for the first time. In a London theater, while standing in the wings, he caught sight of a young and beautiful dancer named Hetty Kelly. Coming offstage, she asked Chaplin to hold her mirror so she could fix her hair. As he stood next to her, admiring her beauty, he felt a strange passion overtake him. The effect, he later said, was bewitching.

Within a matter of days, he had fallen hopelessly in love with Hetty, who was only fifteen. One evening, they dined at a fancy restaurant, but Hetty was uncomfortable during the meal. She did not understand the intensity of Chaplin's emotion and a few days later broke off the affair, leaving Chaplin devastated. Twenty years later, he was still thinking about Hetty, still trying to understand why the relationship had failed. The episode, he came to realize, had been nothing "but a childish infatuation to her, but to me it was the beginning of a spiritual development, a reaching out for beauty."[5]

Attempting to forget his grief, Chaplin forced himself

to concentrate on his stage career. In the autumn of 1909, he and his colleagues traveled to Paris, where they appeared at the Folies-Bergère music hall. One night, after his performance, he was approached by an interpreter, who explained that composer Claude Debussy was in the house and would very much like to meet him. Would he pay a visit to the Frenchman's box?

The meeting that followed was brief but memorable. After expressing surprise that Chaplin was so young, the French composer congratulated him on his graceful performance. "You are instinctively a musician and a dancer," he said. In the years to come, hundreds of film critics would echo Debussy's sentiment.

By 1910, Chaplin had learned so much that Fred Karno offered him the starring role in a new piece, *Jimmy the Fearless*. In the sketch, a boy named Jimmy falls asleep while reading a dime-store novel and, in his dreams, has a series of wild adventures in the Rocky Mountains. It was an exciting role, and Chaplin's vigorous performance was praised by the critics. "His entrance alone," said the *Yorkshire Evening Post*, "sets the house in a roar and stamps him as a born comedian."

While the sketch was touring the provinces, the manager of Karno's American company, Alf Reeves, happened to be in England. With Karno's help, Reeves was putting together a new cast to take with him to the United States, and one evening he went to see *Jimmy the Fearless*. He liked what he saw, especially a clever bit where Chaplin cut into a loaf of bread without glancing up from the book he was reading. "The next thing I knew," Reeves said, "he had carved that loaf into the shape of a concertina."

The following morning, Reeves told Karno that he wanted to bring *Jimmy the Fearless* to the United States, but Karno thought it was a poor idea. Instead, he assigned Reeves a new sketch, *The Wow-Wows*, a spoof of secret societies and their sometimes bizarre initiation ceremonies. Reeves complained that the act was paper-thin, but Karno assured him it would be a big hit in the United States.

After reading the script, Chaplin agreed with Reeves—*The Wow-Wows* was a terrible sketch. Nevertheless, he was eager to visit America, where he hoped to become a vaudeville star. The arrangements were quickly made, and in September 1910, Alf Reeves and his newly assembled company sailed to America aboard the SS *Cairnrona*. After twelve days at sea, land was sighted in the distance. "I'll never forget . . . what happened next," said one cast member. "Suddenly Charlie ran to the railing, took off his hat, waved it and shouted, 'America, I am coming to conquer you! Every man, woman and child shall have my name on their lips—Charles Spencer Chaplin!' We all booed him affectionately, and he bowed to us very formally and sat down again."[6]

Chaplin's first impression of America was not encouraging. The streets of New York were dirty, he said, and the city seemed intimidating and unfriendly. New Yorkers, he noticed, even spoke differently—faster, with an air of impatience. Chaplin was aware that he tended to speak slowly, so for fear of wasting anyone's time, he said as little as possible.

After a few rehearsals, *The Wow-Wows* opened at the Colonial Theatre on October 3. Despite Karno's certainty that it would be a hit, the first-night audience was restless and bored. The show was panned by the press, which dismissed the cast as "the most remarkable collection of blithering, blathering Englishmen New York has seen in many a day." Chaplin's performance, however, was not completely overlooked. "His manner is quiet and easy," said *Variety*, "and he goes about his work in a devil-may-care manner. . . . Chaplin will do all right for America, but it is too bad that he didn't first appear in New York" in something more substantial than *The Wow-Wows*.[7]

Though business picked up a little during the third week, the show was clearly a failure. The cast was preparing to sail back to England when, to everyone's surprise, they received an offer to tour the country for twenty weeks on the Sullivan and Considine circuit. "It was cheap

This 1914 photo reveals a young, pensive Charlie Chaplin.

vaudeville," said Chaplin, but at least the work was steady—three shows a day, $75 a week. As usual, most of Chaplin's salary went right into the bank.

Shortly after the tour began, the players decided to resurrect an old Karno standby, *Mumming Birds* (known in America as *A Night in an English Music Hall*). It was a much funnier sketch than *The Wow-Wows*, and the twenty-week tour was a rousing success. In Butte, Montana, Chaplin was pleased to read that he was "one of the best pantomime artists ever seen here." Slowly but surely, he was beginning to make a name for himself in America.

Like every vaudevillian, Chaplin spent many long hours on the train. To pass the time, the Karno clowns swapped stories, told jokes, and played games like gin rummy and charades. Chaplin, on the other hand, spent his time reading books, studying yoga, or practicing the violin. This convinced his colleagues that he was peculiar, an impression that was supported by his roommate, comedian Stan Laurel. Chaplin, he recalled, "was very moody and often very shabby in appearance. Then suddenly he would astonish us all by getting dressed to kill. . . . We never knew what he was going to do next. He was unpredictable."[8]

In the spring of 1911, the cast returned to New York to stage *A Night in an English Music Hall*. This time, the New York reception was enthusiastic. In the sketch, Chaplin played the part of a well-dressed drunk who proceeds, in hilarious fashion, to disrupt an English variety show. At one point, while attempting to light his cigar, he tumbles out of his box seat onto the stage, where he ends up wrestling with "Marconi Ali, the Terrible Turk." Chaplin was twenty-two years old and his body was surprisingly agile. His pratfalls, said one critic, were breathtaking, "and were he not a skilled acrobat, he would break his neck."

Chaplin's drunk act earned him a large and enthusiastic following; by 1913, he was being referred to as "the biggest laughmaker on the vaudeville stage." Yet, despite his success, he was troubled by a growing sense of restlessness and depression. He was sick and tired of what he called "tenth-rate vaudeville" and its whole drab existence—the shabby hotel rooms, the poor food, the chronic fatigue, the loneliness. After more than five years on the road, Chaplin was ready for a change.

In May 1913, the Karno Company was enjoying a week's layover in Philadelphia when Alf Reeves received an unusual telegram: "IS THERE A MAN NAMED CHAFFIN IN YOUR COMPANY OR SOMETHING LIKE THAT STOP IF SO WILL HE COMMUNICATE WITH KESSEL AND BAUMANN 24 LONGACRE BUILDING BROADWAY NEW YORK."[9]

Charlie (front left) performs with the Karno Company, an English vaudeville troupe.

As Chaplin would soon discover, Adam Kessel and Charles Baumann were the owners of the New York Motion Picture Company. One branch of that company was Keystone, which specialized in slapstick comedy. When Chaplin arrived at the Longacre Building, Kessel surprised him by asking if he would like to be a Keystone actor. Like most comedians, Chaplin was familiar with Keystone's one- and two-reelers. Overall, he didn't care for the studio's zany brand of humor, though he did admire pretty Mabel Normand, Keystone's biggest female star.

At that time, Mack Sennett was Keystone's most celebrated director. Six months earlier in New York, Sennett had seen Chaplin's drunk act, and now he wanted the English comedian to come to California to appear in some of his films. To sweeten the deal, Kessel offered Chaplin an irresistible salary—$150 per week, twice what he was earning with Karno.

It was a tough decision for Chaplin. He realized, on the one hand, that he was being asked to give up the security of vaudeville for an uncertain future in Hollywood. On the other hand, he recognized the publicity value of appearing in motion pictures. "A year at that racket," he said, "and I could return to vaudeville an international star."[10] After thinking it over for several months, Chaplin signed with Keystone in late September.

Before leaving the Karno Company, he had to finish yet another cross-country tour, which ended on November 28. That night, after the show, Alf Reeves accompanied Chaplin to the Kansas City railroad depot. Before boarding the train, Chaplin handed his manager a small package. "Merry Christmas, Alf," he said. After the train had departed, Reeves discovered that Chaplin had given him a new wallet, inside of which he found a $100 bill, along with a handwritten note: "A little tribute to our friendship. To Alf, from Charlie." Reeves kept the wallet—and the note—for many years thereafter.

4

THE LITTLE TRAMP

CHARLIE CHAPLIN ARRIVED IN Los Angeles in early December 1913. After taking a small room at the Great Northern Hotel, he decided to attend the evening show at the Empress Theater, where he happened to meet his new boss, Mack Sennett. The director was disappointed to learn that his new comic was only twenty-four. The man he had seen onstage in New York, he recalled, was an "experienced, knockabout, roughneck, middle-aged comedian. . . . In Los Angeles I met a boy."[1] After dropping Chaplin off at his hotel, Sennett told him to report for work as soon as he could.

A few days later, the comedian made his way to the Keystone Studio in Edendale, a squalid, semi-industrial area east of Los Angeles. He was greeted warmly by Sennett, who encouraged him to spend the next few days exploring the lot and getting to know the other actors. Sennett did his best to put the newcomer at ease, but Chaplin soon felt overwhelmed by the frantic pace at Keystone. The studio, he would discover, was a noisy, slam-bang world of custard pies, fire hoses, folding beds, sink-ing boats, breakaway bottles, and daredevil stunts. If there was a method to the madness, Chaplin could not see it. He felt uneasy in this environment, unsure of himself. By contrast, the Karno Company seemed downright peaceful.

As Sennett walked Chaplin around the lot, he explained how movies were made at Keystone. There were no scripts, the director said: "We get an idea, then follow the natural sequence of events until it leads up to a chase, which is the essence of our comedy."[2] Chaplin listened doubtfully. As an actor, he disliked chases, which he thought tended to flatten out a character's personality. But Sennett was not interested in what Chaplin liked or disliked. The young Englishman was being paid $150 per week, and he would do as he was told.

A crude and overbearing man, Sennett had no illusions about the movie business. He believed that the average filmgoer had the attention span of an eleven-year-old, and he made his comedies accordingly. Speed and action meant everything at Keystone, even if logic had to be tossed out the window. As Sennett warned his comics, "Once we stop to let anybody analyze us, we're sunk."

Chaplin's first film was a one-reeler called *Making a Living*, in which he played a dishonest man trying to get a job as a newspaper reporter. According to Sennett, Chaplin was thoroughly confused during the three-day shoot: "He couldn't understand what was going on, why everything went so fast, and why scenes were shot out of chronology."[3]

Later, when Chaplin saw *Making a Living*, he was heartbroken. Many of his funniest gags had been deleted or ruined by haphazard editing. Nor was Sennett pleased. Everything about Chaplin, he declared, was wrong—his makeup, his costume, his timing, his character. Clearly, something had to be done, but no one at Keystone knew how to remedy the problem.

A day or two later, Sennett was shooting another one-reeler, *Mabel's Strange Predicament*. One of the sequences took place in a hotel lobby. Turning to Chaplin, Sennett told him to put on a funny costume. Anything, he said, would do.

Chaplin hurried back to the men's dressing room, where comedians Ford Sterling, Chester Conklin, and Fatty Arbuckle were absorbed in a game of pinochle. Conklin vividly remembered what happened next: "Charlie ambled about the room looking pale and worried. Arbuckle's trousers were hanging on a chair. . . . Charlie fingered the pants.

"'Mind?'

"Arbuckle didn't mind. Charlie got into the pants. He was a sight and we laughed at him. Poor guy, I guess that was the first time anyone had laughed at him since he closed his music hall act."[4]

The rest of the outfit came together quickly: a pair of oversize shoes, a tight coat, a derby, and a wobbly cane that seemed to come alive in Chaplin's hands. Using a greasepaint pencil, he carefully outlined his eyes. Then, with a dab of spirit gum, he fixed a small mustache to his upper lip.

By now, the game of pinochle had stopped; the other comics were watching Chaplin with interest. "You got something there," one of them said. "Looks like just what you need."

After a final glance in the mirror, Chaplin hurried back to the set, where Sennett was waiting. The director laughed when he saw the preposterous getup. Reassured, Chaplin began to describe the character he had created. He might be a down-and-out tramp, but he was also "a gentleman, a poet, a dreamer, a lonely fellow, always hopeful of romance and adventure." Sennett listened, amused. "All right," he said, "get on the set and see what you can do there."

Swinging his cane in a jaunty manner, Chaplin entered the hotel lobby and promptly tripped over the leash of a dog. "I turned and raised my hat apologetically," he said, "then turned and stumbled over a cuspidor, then turned and raised my hat to the cuspidor." Behind the camera, the crew began to laugh. Soon a crowd had gathered to watch Chaplin rehearse. No one realized it at the time, but the character he had created, the Little Tramp, would become the most recognizable, most beloved character in movie history.

"I felt he was a reality, a living person," Chaplin wrote. "In fact he ignited all sorts of crazy ideas that I would never have dreamt of, until I was dressed and made up as the Tramp."[5]

Chaplin spent one year at Keystone, where he appeared in thirty-four short films and one feature-length production. He proved to be a quick learner, and before long he had mastered many of the fundamentals of moviemaking. He watched, he listened, he asked questions; after work, he went to the cutting room to observe how films were spliced together, scene by scene. He studied lighting and camera placement; gradually, he learned how to use title cards and editing to speed up the action. "It was so free and easy," he said, "no literature, no writers—we just had a notion around which we built gags, then made up the story as we went along."[6]

By the spring of 1914, Chaplin felt he was ready to direct his own one-reelers. Reluctantly, Sennett gave him the go-ahead, warning him not to spend more than $1,000 on any production. The first two comedies that Chaplin directed were *Twenty Minutes of Love* and *Caught in the Rain*. Later, he would have little to say about the first film—most likely, he dismissed it as the work of a beginner—but he was very proud of *Caught in the Rain*, which was released on May 4. "It was not a world-beater," he admitted, "but it was funny and quite a success." Another comedy from this period was *His Favorite Pastime*, in which Chaplin demonstrated his remarkable athletic ability. Playing a drunk, he somersaults off a balcony, yet manages to land on a sofa sitting right-side up—still smoking his cigarette! It's a quick gag, one that is easy to miss. For those viewers who catch it, however, it is an astonishing trick, one that must have taken many hours to perfect.

By midsummer, Chaplin was turning out a steady succession of one- and two-reel comedies: *The Knockout, The Fatal Mallet, The Property Man, The New Janitor, Laughing Gas, Recreation.* He enjoyed the challenge of completing a new film every week and was delighted when audiences began to recognize him on the screen. Soon Sennett was receiving orders from New York to "hurry up with more Chaplin pictures as there [is] a terrific demand for them."

Chaplin's twenty-ninth film for Keystone was a two-reeler called *Dough and Dynamite.* A lively romp set in a bakery, it took nine days to shoot and grossed more than $130,000 the first year of its release. It was this film, said Sennett, that established Chaplin as an important motion picture comedian.

On the evening of August 9, 1914, Chaplin wrote a letter to his brother, Sydney, who was still working for the Karno Company. World War I had just broken out a few days earlier, but in his letter Charlie showed little interest in the European conflict. Instead, he was eager to tell Sydney about his film work and how well his career was going: "All the theatres feature my name in big letters. . . . I tell you in this country I am a big box office attraction. . . . I have 50 [fan] letters a week . . . and next year I hope to make a bunch of dough."

In his letter, Charlie encouraged his brother to leave England and come to Edendale, where he could help him get an acting job at Keystone: "You will like it out hear [*sic*] it is a beautiful country and the fresh air is doing me the world of good." After expressing the hope that Sydney wouldn't have to fight in the war, Charlie closed his letter with another bit of movie news: "I have just finished a six real [*sic*] picture with Marie Dressler. . . . It is the best thing I ever did."[7]

The project he was referring to was *Tillie's Punctured Romance,* a comedy directed by Mack Sennett. By today's standards, it is not a particularly funny film, but historically it is important: at six reels (eighty minutes), it was the first feature-length comedy. Released in November 1914, it went on to become one of the biggest box-office hits of the year.

The star of *Tillie's Punctured Romance* was Marie Dressler, but according to Sennett, the film "benefited Charlie Chaplin more than anyone else. . . . After this picture every producer was after him." Therefore, when it

Charlie appears in Tillie's Punctured Romance *(1914) with Marie Dressler (center) and Mabel Normand. The 80-minute film was the first feature-length comedy ever produced, and its success helped make Chaplin a star.*

came time to renew Chaplin's contract, Sennett offered him $750 per week, but Chaplin held out for more. Boldly, he asked for $1,000 per week. Sennett was horrified and refused to discuss the matter any further.

Though it pained him to leave Keystone, Chaplin realized that his future lay elsewhere, and on November 14, 1914, he signed a one-year contract with the Essanay Film Company, headquartered in Chicago. Essanay's terms were extremely generous: $1,250 per week, plus a bonus of $10,000 for signing. "I was elated," said the comedian. "It seemed too good to be true."

After editing his final Keystone picture, Chaplin took the train east to Chicago. Upon his arrival at the Essanay studio, he was told to report to the head of the scenario department, Louella Parsons. She would give him a script to direct. In an irritated tone of voice, Chaplin made it clear that he wouldn't be needing Miss Parsons's help. He preferred to write his own stories. He was soon at work gathering ideas for a two-reel comedy, aptly titled *His New Job*.

There were a number of talented people employed at Essanay, and before shooting began, Chaplin was told by the casting office that he could select anyone to play his leading lady. One of the young women he interviewed was Gloria Swanson, an attractive teenager who was just getting her start in motion pictures (she would later become one of the silent screen's best-known actresses).

Though she was only fifteen, Swanson believed that she should be playing dramatic roles, and she was dismayed when Chaplin asked her to be his partner. They spent one entire morning, she recalled, trying to work up comic routines: "These all involved kicking each other in the pants, running into things, and falling over each other. He kept laughing . . . and encouraging me to let myself go and be silly." She tried to give Chaplin what he wanted, but "for the life of me," she said, "I couldn't get the feel of his frisky little skits. . . . I felt like a cow trying to dance with a toy poodle."

At Keystone's third-anniversary party in 1915, Charlie visits with (left to right) producer-director Tom Ince, Mack Sennett, and legendary director D. W. Griffith.

The next morning, Swanson learned that Chaplin had selected someone else to play opposite him. Instead of feeling disappointed, she wrote, "I was absolutely delighted. . . . I would have been mortified if anybody I knew had ever seen me get kicked in the pants . . . by an odd sprite in a hobo outfit."[8]

His New Job was the only film Chaplin directed at the Essanay studio in Chicago. He couldn't warm up to the people who worked there, nor did he entirely trust George Spoor, one of the two owners of the company. Chaplin feared that if he stayed in Chicago, his creativity would be undermined by Spoor's penny-pinching mentality. As soon as he could arrange it, he took the train west to Niles, California, where Essanay produced a series of popular Westerns starring "Broncho Billy" Anderson. Though he found the studio primitive and ill equipped, it was here, in the small town of Niles, that Chaplin began to show significant growth as an artist.

His first task was to pull together a production unit: some carpenters, an electrician, a wardrobe person, a makeup artist, one or two gag writers, a cameraman, an assistant director, and a small supporting cast. He also had to find a suitable leading lady, a frustrating experience because there were so few actresses to choose from. Then, by chance, he heard about an attractive young stenographer named Edna Purviance, who lived in San Francisco. "She was more than pretty," said Chaplin, "she was beautiful." Blonde and delicate, passive by nature, Purviance had a certain melancholy about her that the young filmmaker found irresistible. Chaplin hired her on the spot.

Unfortunately, acting was not one of Purviance's natural gifts. She made mistakes and her first few performances were awkward and self-conscious. But Chaplin was patient, carefully explaining what he wanted her to do and showing her the appropriate expressions and movements for each scene. In this painstaking way, Purviance learned her craft, and over the next eight years she and Chaplin would appear together in thirty-five films. They fell in love almost immediately, and as time passed Chaplin began to allow elements of romance to creep into his one- and two-reel comedies. This not only widened their appeal, but helped make the Little Tramp a gentler and more sympathetic character than he had been at Keystone. Chaplin, the public learned, could be as touching as he was funny.

Dramatically, *The Bank* and *The Tramp* are the two most interesting pictures Chaplin made for Essanay. In each case, the Little Tramp falls in love with a woman (played by Purviance) who cannot, or will not, return his love. In *The Bank*, Edna tosses out a pretty bouquet of flowers that

Charlie, the janitor, has given her. Crushed, he retreats to his corner, where he falls asleep and dreams that the bank is being robbed. Courageously, he foils the robbery and saves Edna. At the end of the dream, the janitor happily takes Edna into his arms; at that moment, he wakes up to find himself kissing his mop. "The situation is poignant and it is funny," says writer John McCabe. "It is, to use a word which now means both of those things together, Chaplinesque."[9]

The Tramp has a different, but equally effective, ending. After writing Edna a farewell note, Charlie trudges unhappily down the road, cane bent, shoulders sunk. Then, gradually, he appears to recover his spirits. He shrugs and kicks his heels up. His step becomes brighter. Though temporarily dismayed, the Little Tramp refuses to give in to despair. He knows—and the audience knows—that there is always the hope of tomorrow.

The idea of mixing comedy with pathos had already been perfected by Fred Karno, but, curiously, it had not yet been attempted on the screen. It was a combination, however, that perfectly suited the lonely, wistful character of the Little Tramp. As one Chaplin biographer has noted, "A comedy with a sad end was something new. . . . It was from this time that serious critics . . . began to discover what the common public had long ago recognized, that Chaplin was not like anyone else before him."[10]

After making a handful of films at Niles, Chaplin convinced Essanay to send him back to Los Angeles, where he rented a small studio near the center of town. Here he made another half-dozen films, all of which did extremely well at the box office.

Though his pictures were gradually becoming more serious, slapstick comedy was still the order of the day. In *Work*, the Little Tramp creates havoc while attempting to decorate a house (lots of gags involving ladders and wallpaper paste); in *A Jitney Elopement*, Chaplin recreates the little gag that had so delighted Alf Reeves in *Jimmy the Fear-*

less, absentmindedly cutting a bread roll into the shape of a concertina. In *The Champion*, two prizefighters slug it out in the ring, the entire bout choreographed like an elaborate dance (at one point, hilariously, the two boxers break into a fox-trot).

The fourteen films that Chaplin made for Essanay were not only financially successful; they also established him as the most popular comedian in the United States. By the end of 1915, millions of Americans had become obsessed with Charlie, the Little Tramp. The craze was dubbed "Chaplinitis" and, for a while, it was impossible to escape. There were Charlie Chaplin costumes, squirt rings, dolls, comic strips, buttons, posters, and a number of popular songs and dances. In New York, at the fashionable *Ziegfeld Follies*, chorus girls donned mustaches and baggy pants to perform a humorous number, "Those Charlie Chaplin Feet."

By this time, Sydney had also moved to America. He worked for a while as a comic at Keystone; then, with the advent of "Chaplinitis," he quit acting to devote himself full-time to his brother's increasingly complicated business affairs. When Essanay began to discuss the renewal of Chaplin's contract, it was Sydney who handled the negotiations. Eager to retain Chaplin's services, Essanay offered him $350,000 to appear in twelve two-reel pictures. This was big money, and Chaplin was inclined to say yes. But Sydney told him to wait. If Essanay was willing to pay that much, he said, another studio might be willing to pay more. After instructing his brother not to sign a contract with anyone, Sydney went to New York to field offers.

While there, he met with representatives from several motion picture studios, including Fox and Universal. In the end, the Mutual Film Corporation offered the most attractive terms: $10,000 per week, plus a bonus of $150,000. It was a dazzling and unprecedented sum. As one publicist observed, "Next to the war in Europe Chaplin is the most expensive item in contemporaneous history."[11]

*In 1917, Charlie holds up a Little Tramp doll, a testament to
the popularity of his screen character. Through the Little Tramp
—a wistful, invincible vagabond—Chaplin eloquently combined
comedy and pathos.*

The signing of the contract took place in New York on February 26, 1916. Motion picture cameras were there to record the historic event. "That evening," Chaplin recalled, "I stood with the crowd in Times Square as the news flashed on the electric sign that ran around the Times Building. It read: 'Chaplin signs with Mutual at $670,000 a year.' I stood and read it objectively as though it were about someone else. So much had happened to me, my emotions were spent."[12]

5
REEL LIFE

IN MARCH 1916, CHARLIE CHAPLIN returned to Los Angeles to begin work on his first film for Mutual, *The Floorwalker*. Set in a well-stocked department store, the two-reeler featured a number of clever sequences, including a wild and breathless chase on an escalator. (When Mack Sennett saw the film, he was heard to exclaim, "Why the hell didn't *we* ever think of a running staircase?")

The Floorwalker was released to acclaim in May 1916. The same month, *Harper's Weekly* published an article entitled "The Art of Charles Chaplin." It was written by a prominent stage actress, Minnie Maddern Fiske. In her essay, Fiske praised Chaplin for his "inexhaustible imagination" and "perfect technique." He was to be applauded, she said, "for making irresistible entertainment out of more or less worthless material." Some of Chaplin's humor, she admitted, "is vulgar . . . [but] vulgarity and distinguished art can exist together. . . . Those of us who believe that Charles Chaplin is essentially a great comic artist look forward to fine achievements." Fiske's article was widely read and commented upon. It helped the public to see Chaplin in a new light—not just as a gifted clown, but as a cinematic genius.

"It is said he came from a life of sadness," Fiske concluded. "And at twenty-six he has made the world laugh. Quite a beautiful thing to do!"[1]

It was during this same period, in mid-1916, that Chaplin's loyalty to Great Britain was called into question. According to his Mutual contract, he could not leave the United States without his employers' permission. The insertion of this clause was probably an attempt on Mutual's part to prevent Chaplin from being drafted (or to at least hinder the process). When this item was reported in the British press, the comedian began to receive hundreds of letters from England accusing him of being a "slacker." Some of the envelopes contained white feathers, a symbol of cowardice during the war. To prove his patriotism, Chaplin registered for the draft. He also contributed a large sum of money to the British war cause. But there were still a number of people in Britain who considered him something of a coward.

After completing *The Floorwalker*, Chaplin went on to make eleven more films for Mutual, including *One A.M., The Pawnshop, The Rink, The Cure,* and *Easy Street.* According to biographer Theodore Huff, the eighteen months that Chaplin spent at Mutual were his "most fertile years, his most sustained creative period." Compared to the one- and two-reelers made for Essanay, the Mutual films represent the full blossoming of Chaplin's comedic talents. As many critics have pointed out, never again would his pictures be so consistently funny or so lighthearted in tone.

Perhaps the most unusual film from this period was *One A.M.,* in which Chaplin appeared solo, playing a drunk returning home after a night on the town. After encountering numerous obstacles in the house, he does furious battle with a stubborn folding bed. Repeatedly, the bed refuses to cooperate, snapping back into the wall, turning upside down, bucking like a bronco when Chaplin attempts to "ride" it. Some critics have complained that the sequence goes on too long; nevertheless, it is an inspired and hilarious bit of filmmaking. *One A.M.*, says Theodore Huff, "is a rare piece of virtuosity, a tour de force in which Chaplin successfully holds the screen with pantomime alone for two reels."[2]

Unlike most comedians, Chaplin was a perfectionist when it came to directing. He would often shoot a scene twenty or thirty times before he was satisfied. This, according to one biographer, "was something new in Hollywood. For most directors, shots were only retaken if something had gone noticeably wrong. . . . [To] shoot any scene more than once would have been an admission of inadequate rehearsal and error. For Chaplin it was an assertion that it was always possible to do better."[3]

One of the cleverest films Chaplin made for Mutual was *The Pawnshop*, released in October 1916. Halfway through the film, a customer enters the shop and hands Charlie an alarm clock, which he hopes to pawn. Charlie, however, must examine it first. He begins by listening to the clock with a stethoscope. Dissatisfied, he cuts it open with a can opener, then sniffs the contents as though it were a tin of sardines. Like a doctor, he pokes, he prods; using a pair of dental forceps, he performs a necessary extraction. He removes the mainspring, measures it, then begins to snip off bits, as though it were a length of ribbon. In no time at all, Charlie has reduced a perfectly good clock to a useless pile of junk.

"The imagination is accurate," said one critic. "The acting is restrained and naturalistic. The result is a scream."

Though most of his Mutual films concentrate on fast action and slapstick humor, Chaplin occasionally touched upon more serious themes. In the two-reeler *Easy Street*, he plays a policeman assigned to clean up one of the toughest sections of town. While making his rounds, he encounters brief but graphic examples of poverty, starvation, drug addiction, and urban violence. By incorporating such images, Chaplin was not trying to shock or depress the public; nor was he demanding social reform. He was simply introducing elements of realism and drama that would become increasingly important to him as a filmmaker.

By the time *Easy Street* was released in early 1917, Chaplin had assembled a stock company of performers, many of whom would remain on his payroll for years. Besides Edna Purviance, the comedians included Albert Austin, Leo White, Charlotte Mineau, Henry Bergman, Loyal Underwood, and fierce-looking Eric Campbell, who usually played the "heavy" (the angry store manager, the town bully, the intimidating head waiter). It was also during this period that Chaplin hired a young cameraman named Roland "Rollie" Totheroh, whom he had met at the Essanay Studio in Niles. A capable, if undistinguished, cinematographer, Totheroh would continue to work for the director until 1952.

The year and a half that Chaplin spent at Mutual was probably the happiest period of his career. "I was light and unencumbered," he said, "twenty-seven years old, with fabulous prospects and a friendly, glamorous world before me. Within a short time I would be a millionaire—it all seemed slightly mad."[4]

Though he was now earning a very large salary, Chaplin's lifestyle was surprisingly modest. He showed no interest in buying a Hollywood mansion, preferring instead to occupy a room at the Los Angeles Athletic Club for $12 a week. Most evenings, he dined quietly at the club, usually with Edna Purviance, who continued to be his closest companion. Chaplin assumed that someday they would marry, but much to his regret, he never got around to proposing. Edna, feeling neglected, eventually fell in love with another actor, Thomas Meighan.

"I could not believe it," said Chaplin. "My pride was hurt; I was outraged." But he knew in his heart that he had only himself to blame.

One of Chaplin's last films for Mutual was *The Immigrant*, in which he again mixed slapstick comedy with moments of genuine pathos. The story concerned two immigrants (Charlie and Edna) who are among the many passengers on a ship bound for America. Early on, Edna's meager savings are stolen by a thief; Charlie, who has just won a tidy sum in a game of poker, quietly slips some money into Edna's pocket. When she discovers what he has done, she tearfully thanks him.

After a long and turbulent voyage, Charlie catches sight of the Statue of Liberty. Instantly, two officials rush forward, roping the immigrants together like a herd of cattle. Struggling behind the rope barrier, Charlie casts a quizzical glance at the famed statue. The irony of the situation is clear: this is liberty?

Upon disembarking, Charlie and Edna go their separate ways. Later, they meet again in a café. Both are nearly penniless, and Charlie has trouble paying the bill. At this very moment, they are approached by an artist, who offers them money if Edna will pose for him. Thinking quickly, Charlie asks for and receives a two-dollar advance. It is the first stroke of luck he and Edna have enjoyed since stepping off the boat.

Happily, they leave the café. Outside, it is raining, but Charlie refuses to let the weather dampen his spirits. Sweeping Edna into his arms, he carries her through the door of the nearest marriage license bureau. It is a sweet and hopeful ending; despite all the problems the pair have endured, a spirit of optimism prevails. Charlie and Edna may be poor, and their future may be doubtful, but they have each other—and that is enough.

"*The Immigrant*," said Chaplin, "touched me more than any other film I made. I thought the end had quite a poetic feeling." Today critics agree that it is one of his most impressive two-reelers. "Of all his early work," writes Isabel Quigley, "[*The Immigrant*] came closest to his darker and more directly satirical films of the late twenties and thirties."[5]

Charlie and Edna Purviance star in The Immigrant *(1917). Between 1915 and 1923, Chaplin cast Purviance as the leading lady in most of his films.*

While *The Immigrant* was in production, Sydney was negotiating a new contract for his brother. The president of Mutual was prepared to offer Chaplin $1 million to star in eight two-reel comedies. Chaplin's association with Mutual had been a happy one, but as Sydney explained to the press, he and his brother were in no hurry to sign a contract. "All the big film companies are now negotiating with me for Charlie's services," he said, "and I am just waiting for the best offer."[6]

Shortly after that, Sydney was approached by the directors of a brand-new company, First National, who offered

Chaplin $1 million to produce eight two-reel comedies. The terms were more than fair. For each film that Chaplin made, First National would advance him $125,000. As an independent producer, Chaplin would have to cover all costs of filming, but the financial rewards were great: after all expenses had been recovered, he and First National would split the profits from each film evenly. The comedian was also promised more creative control than he had enjoyed at either Essanay or Mutual. After a lengthy period of negotiation, Chaplin signed with First National in June 1917.

He spent the balance of the summer shooting *The Adventurer*, his final comedy for Mutual. Then, in late August, he took a much-needed vacation to the Hawaiian Islands. The weather was beautiful and the foliage lush, but Chaplin found it hard to relax. In Hawaii, he said, "I felt a subtle claustrophobia, as if imprisoned inside a lily." After five weeks of sun and surf, he sailed back to California, eager to return to work.

A month later, in October, he began building a new, state-of-the-art studio on the outskirts of Hollywood. Occupying five acres, it contained a large, open-air stage, dozens of dressing rooms and workshops, a swimming pool, stables, a tennis court, a garden, and a ten-room house where Sydney lived with his wife, Minnie. To oversee daily operations, Chaplin hired his old friend Alf Reeves, who was still working for the Karno Company. Reeves arrived at the Chaplin Studio in January 1918; by April, he had taken over as general manager, a post he would occupy for the next twenty-eight years.

The studio was still under construction when Chaplin began work on *A Dog's Life*, his first film as an independent producer. One of his most poignant comedies, it paralleled the lives of two unfortunates: a homeless tramp and a stray dog who manage to help each other in delightful and unexpected ways. Chaplin also inserted a second, more serious story involving an unhappy singer, with

Edna and Charlie hold their co-star in this publicity shot for
A Dog's Life *(1918), Chaplin's first film as an independent producer.*

whom the Little Tramp falls in love. Released in April 1918, *A Dog's Life* was warmly praised for its skillful blend of slapstick humor and realistic drama. *Photoplay* magazine called it one of the year's finest achievements; French critic Louis Delluc would later pronounce it "the cinema's first total work of art."

Shortly before the film's release, Chaplin was invited to a party given by producer Samuel Goldwyn. There he met a sixteen-year-old actress named Mildred Harris. Blonde and blue-eyed, she was extremely pretty, and Chaplin enjoyed her company. Like every young actress, Mildred knew that Chaplin was the most eligible bachelor in Hollywood and, over the next several weeks, she did everything she could to make herself agreeable to the twenty-nine-year-old director. Soon they were dating on a steady basis.

The mood in Hollywood, meanwhile, had turned unusually serious. Everyone was talking about the war in Europe and the terrible toll it was taking. Countless soldiers had lost their lives on the battlefields, and in April, Chaplin was asked to go to Washington, D.C., to inaugurate the third Liberty Bond campaign. Joining him on the tour were Douglas Fairbanks and Mary Pickford, two of Hollywood's most popular screen idols.

In Washington, Chaplin delivered a vigorous speech, imploring the crowd to buy bonds to raise money for the Allied cause. "The Germans are at your door!" he shouted. "We've got to stop them! And we *will* stop them if you buy Liberty Bonds!" At a subsequent rally in New York, he, Fairbanks, and Pickford sold more than $2 million worth of bonds to a large, cheering crowd.

Upon his return to Los Angeles in May, Chaplin embarked on a new film, *Shoulder Arms*, a three-reel comedy about a soldier's misadventures during the war. From the start, Chaplin's friends felt uneasy about the project. It was dangerous, they told him, to satirize the war, and when he finished the picture that fall, he wondered if they were right. In the film, he had depicted the typical hardships suffered by soldiers during wartime—hunger, homesickness, cold weather, stale food, and waterlogged trenches. It was all presented in a humorous way, but Chaplin began to fear that the public might take offense. In a creative panic, he considered scrapping the film altogether.

Fortunately, his friend Douglas Fairbanks asked to see it. Nervously, Chaplin consented. In the screening room, Fairbanks laughed so hard that tears streamed from his eyes. Afterwards, he told Chaplin that *Shoulder Arms* was wonderful, one of the funniest films he had ever seen. On the strength of Fairbanks's reaction, Chaplin released *Shoulder Arms* to theaters in October 1918, just three weeks before the war came to an end. To his astonishment, it was a tremendous success with the public, one of the biggest box-office hits of the year.

"It was a film," writes John McCabe, "that said many things to many people; it was by turns bravura slapstick, a realistic image of war's roiling discomforts, sentimental whimsy, and unashamed flag waving."[7] Some aspects of *Shoulder Arms* now seem dated, but in the fall of 1918 it was considered Chaplin's most accomplished work to date, firmly establishing him as one of America's preeminent filmmakers.

His personal life, meanwhile, had taken a drastic turn for the worse. Though he had been dating Mildred Harris only a short while, she now informed him that she was pregnant. Naturally, Chaplin was alarmed. He had worked too hard to have his career destroyed by a sex scandal, and on October 23, 1918, he and Mildred were quietly married at the home of a local registrar. Chaplin was so preoccupied during the ceremony he forgot to kiss the bride.

The marriage, predictably, was not a success. Chaplin had been forced into it and, as time passed, he began to resent Mildred's childish and immature approach to life. "She had no sense of reality," he complained. "I would try to talk seriously to her about our plans, but nothing penetrated. . . . [Her mind] was cluttered with pink-ribboned foolishness."[8]

During this stressful and anxious period, Chaplin's creativity began to suffer. His next film, *Sunnyside*, had some lyrical moments, but overall it was a disappointment. When it was released in June 1919, the critics did not hesitate to give it bad reviews. "Is the Chaplin Vogue Passing?" a magazine article dared to ask.

A few weeks later, on July 7, Mildred gave birth to a son, Norman Spencer Chaplin. Tragically, the baby was born deformed and died three days later, on July 10. Chaplin was devastated by the death of his son. "Charlie took it hard," said Mildred. "That's the only thing I can

In 1918, Charlie married sixteen-year-old Mildred Harris (pictured here in 1920). They were divorced two years later.

remember about Charlie . . . that he cried when the baby died."[9]

In his autobiography, Chaplin would call this one of the darkest periods of his life. He could see that his marriage was failing; often, he said, "I would come home to find the dinner table laid for one, and would eat alone." Nor was his film work bringing him any satisfaction. That fall, he managed to finish a new picture, *A Day's Pleasure*, but it was hardly worth the effort. A bland comedy about a family's outing on an excursion boat, it did nothing to enhance his reputation as a cinematic genius.

Shortly after the film's release in December, Chaplin and his wife agreed to separate. They had become strangers to each other and saw no reason to continue the charade of a happy marriage. In August 1920, Mildred filed for divorce, declaring that she had suffered "great mental anguish" during the marriage. She also claimed that she had been deserted by her husband, who earlier that year had moved back to the Los Angeles Athletic Club.

"I never knew where [Charlie] was or what he was doing," Mildred told reporters. "He married me, and as soon as he married me he forgot all about me."[10]

⑥
BACK ON TOP

IN JULY 1919, JUST TWO WEEKS after the death of his infant son, Charlie Chaplin began work on his most ambitious project to date, a six-reel picture called *The Kid*. His first feature-length film, it would not only revitalize his career, but would once again demonstrate his mastery at blending slapstick comedy with scenes of genuine pathos. "A single misstep might have made it mawkish," says Theodore Huff, "but no such misstep was made."[1]

In the film, Chaplin appeared as the Little Tramp, but the real star of *The Kid* was a lively boy named Jackie Coogan, whom Chaplin had spotted one night at the Orpheum Theater in Los Angeles. Jackie's father, Jack, had been performing there as a dancer; at the end of the act, as Jack was taking his bows, his young son ran onstage to flash a smile, wave, and do an energetic shimmy. Like everyone else in the audience, Chaplin was won over by the little boy's sparkling personality.

A few days later, he happened to see the youngster again, this time at the Alexandria Hotel, where Jackie and his parents were dining. Intrigued, Chaplin walked over and introduced himself to Mr. and Mrs. Coogan. Then, squatting down, he began talking to four-year-old Jackie. Chaplin spent the next ninety minutes playing with the boy in the hotel lobby. Afterwards, he told Mrs. Coogan that her son was "the most amazing person" he'd ever met. Within a short time, Chaplin had signed the boy to a $75 per week film contract. Though he had no particular project in mind, he wasn't about to let such a talented youngster slip through his fingers.

In later years, whenever Jackie Coogan spoke about Chaplin, he would recall him as a kind and patient director, always willing to describe a scene or act out a particular part. He also remembered Chaplin's perfectionism. The director, for example, spent two weeks working on a

Charlie steps behind the camera to direct a scene. As a director and producer, Chaplin spared no cost or effort to assure the quality of his films.

short scene in which the Kid prepares a pancake breakfast. Like many people at the Chaplin Studio, Jackie must have become frustrated by the endless retakes, but he never once complained, approaching his work with professionalism and a contagious sense of fun. "The whole thing," he said, "was like a wonderful game to me."

By turns hilarious and heartbreaking, *The Kid* tells the story of a penniless tramp who discovers an abandoned baby in an alley. Unable to give the child to anyone in the neighborhood, Charlie decides to raise the tyke as his own.

Five years pass, during which Charlie teaches the Kid everything he knows, from table manners to street fighting to matters of personal hygiene (Jackie is first spotted sitting on the curb, cleaning his fingernails). The Tramp and the Kid enjoy a loving relationship, one that is threatened, however, by the sudden appearance of the welfare authorities. Upon learning that the Tramp is not the boy's natural father, the welfare workers take matters into their own hands. Roughly, they throw the screaming, hysterical child onto the back of a truck, declaring that he must be taken away to the county orphanage.

The Tramp, determined to rescue his son, makes a frantic dash across a series of rooftops; then, with perfect timing, he leaps onto the back of the truck, where he clutches Jackie in a passionate, tearful embrace. The sequence is unforgettable, harrowing in its emotional intensity. Were Jackie's tears real, one critic asked, or was he merely acting? If real, "then there are depths in this small soul which frighten me."

Chaplin and his crew spent nearly a year working on *The Kid.* This was an exceptionally long time for a director to spend on a comedy, but Chaplin wouldn't allow himself to be rushed. During that lengthy period, the thirty-three million Americans who went to the movies every week relied upon other comedians to provide them with a steady stream of laughter.

Buster Keaton, for one. A former child star of the vaudeville stage, Keaton was a solemn-faced clown who was beginning to enjoy great success on the screen. He had made his movie debut in 1917 in *The Butcher Boy*, a two-reeler starring Fatty Arbuckle. The athletic twenty-one-year-old was immediately singled out for praise: "Newcomer Keaton can take a fall and still come up swinging for laughs." A nine-month army stint during the war had interrupted his career, but since his return to Los Angeles, Keaton had been turning out one successful short film after another. One of the funniest was *One Week* (1920), in which he played a newlywed trying to build his own home from a do-it-yourself kit. *Motion Picture World* called it "the comedy sensation of the year."

On June 30, 1920, Chaplin finished shooting *The Kid*. He had just begun to edit the picture when his wife, Mildred, filed for divorce. By that time, Chaplin had spent nearly $500,000 producing *The Kid*, and he was fearful that Mildred might try to seize the film as part of their community property. To prevent that from happening, he and his cameraman, Rollie Totheroh, fled by train to Salt Lake City, where they rented a suite at the Salt Lake Hotel. There, in secrecy, they continued to edit *The Kid*.

It was an enormous task. Chaplin and Totheroh had amassed 400,000 feet of exposed film, which now had to be trimmed to six reels (5,250 feet). "We had over two thousand takes to sort out," Chaplin remembered, "and, although they were numbered, one would occasionally get lost and we would be hours searching for it."[2] Aggravating an already stressful situation, the nitrate-based film was highly flammable and had to be handled with care.

In mid-October—while Chaplin was putting the finishing touches on *The Kid*—Fatty Arbuckle released his first feature-length comedy, *The Round Up*. Simultaneously, Metro released Keaton's first feature, *The Saphead*. The latter film was described by the *New York Times* as "one of the gayest comedies of the season. . . . a bubbling source of

In this still from The Kid *(1921), the Little Tramp and the Kid are about to get into big trouble.* The Kid, *the first full-length comedy that Chaplin directed, was a big hit at the box office.*

merriment." Meanwhile, Chaplin's fans were beginning to wonder what had become of him. Nearly a year had passed since the release of his last film, *A Day's Pleasure.* Robert Sherwood, writing in *Life* magazine, summed up the situation: "It is just as well that Charlie Chaplin did not wait any longer before releasing *The Kid,* for otherwise he might have awakened one bright morning to find that his crown had passed to the pensive brow of Buster Keaton."[3]

Fortunately for Chaplin, his first feature-length film was an immediate and overwhelming success. Advertised as "six reels of joy," *The Kid* was released on February 6, 1921. Throughout the world, it was hailed as an artistic triumph, one of the finest motion pictures ever produced. Chaplin, said one reviewer, "can bring tears or laughter to the largest audience in the world with less apparent effort than any other actor on the screen."[4] *The Kid* not only confirmed Chaplin's status as a major filmmaker, but launched the career of young Jackie Coogan, who went on to become the most important child star of the 1920s. "No child actor," wrote David Robinson, "whether in silent or in sound pictures, has ever surpassed Jackie Coogan's performance as The Kid, in its truthfulness and range of sentiment."[5]

Shortly after the film's premiere, in March, the Chaplin brothers arranged to have their mother brought over from England. Hannah, despite years of treatment, had never fully regained her sanity. While crossing the Atlantic, her behavior seemed normal, but upon arriving in New York she mistook the head of immigration for Jesus Christ, which caused a regrettable delay.

In Southern California, Chaplin set up his mother in a comfortable bungalow near the ocean, where she lived until her death in 1928. For the first time in years, Hannah was happy, though she seemed unable to appreciate her son's fame or even to understand the precise nature of his work. One day, while visiting the studio, she saw him dressed in his tramp costume. "Charlie," she said sadly, "I have to get you a new suit."

Chaplin followed up *The Kid* with a modest two-reeler, *The Idle Class,* in which he played two roles—a wealthy alcoholic and a hobo, who happen to look alike. Near the end of the film, their paths cross when the Tramp finds himself at a high-society costume ball, where, naturally, he is mistaken for the socialite. When his identity is at last revealed, the Tramp is forced to take sudden flight (many Chaplin two-reelers end in this fashion). *The Idle Class* was released in September 1921, and though it wasn't nearly as impressive as *The Kid*, it was nevertheless a box-office success.

The Idle Class was Chaplin's sixty-ninth film. He had just begun to shoot his seventieth, *Pay Day*, when he realized how tired he was. Four years had passed since his Hawaiian vacation; it was time, he decided, to close the studio and take a month-long trip to England. "There is only one place to spend a holiday, long overdue," he told the press, "and that is at home. . . . I want to walk the streets, see all the many changes, and feel the good old London atmosphere again."[6]

The comedian's homecoming aroused intense interest throughout Britain. When Chaplin finally arrived on September 9, it was the biggest event in London since the signing of the armistice in 1918. At Waterloo Station, thousands of people assembled on the platform to welcome Chaplin back to the city of his birth. At the Ritz Hotel, where the actor was staying, an even larger crowd gathered beneath the balcony, hoping to catch a glimpse of their idol. Within days, Chaplin had received seventy-three thousand letters, invitations, and congratulatory telegrams. He was the man of the moment, Hollywood's "golden boy." Everyone wanted to be near him.

Chaplin, on the other hand, wanted desperately to be left alone, at least for a few hours. The very afternoon of his arrival, he managed to escape from the Ritz and wander the streets alone, unrecognized. Allowing himself to slip into a melancholy mood, he revisited the scenes of his boyhood: Kennington Gate, where he had romanced

Hetty Kelly, the first girl he had ever loved; Canterbury Music Hall, where, as a boy, he had once seen his father perform; and Baxter Hall, where, he said, "we used to see magic lantern shows for a penny. . . . You could get a cup of coffee and a piece of cake there and see the Crucifixion of Christ all at the same time."[7]

After a brief stay in London, Chaplin traveled to Paris, where throngs of fans lined the streets to greet their beloved "Charlot," as Chaplin was known in France. Then, in late September, he visited the German capital of Berlin, a city still trying to recover from the ravages of the war. While in Berlin, Chaplin was introduced to a glamorous young actress named Pola Negri. In her memoirs, Negri expressed surprise that Chaplin looked nothing at all "like his screen character. He wore no mustache and was going grey. The only physically attractive thing about him were his hands, which were never without a cigarette."[8] Negri was one of Germany's biggest film stars, and during Chaplin's stay in Berlin, she was constantly at his side. According to the comedian, her only English words, which she kept repeating, were "Jazz boy Charlie!"

On October 6, Chaplin returned to Paris, where he was decorated by the French government for his outstanding work as a filmmaker. The following day, he flew back to England, where he spent a relaxing weekend at the country home of author H. G. Wells. Then, feeling rejuvenated, Chaplin boarded a ship bound for New York. His month-long European holiday had been a wonderful experience, but, in his words, the time had come "to return to California and get back to work. . . . I was now entering the last mile of my contract with First National and looking forward to its termination."[9]

For some time now, Chaplin's dealings with First National had been less than satisfactory. The people in charge, he complained, were "unsympathetic and short-sighted." They were also, in his opinion, unusually stingy. On several occasions, Chaplin had asked the board to advance him more money, explaining that his films were costing more to produce than he had anticipated—but this request always fell upon deaf ears. "You've signed a contract," the comedian was told, "and we expect you to live up to it."

Chaplin should not have been surprised by this attitude. It was, after all, common knowledge that he had no intention of renewing his contract with First National. Two years earlier, screen star Douglas Fairbanks had announced to the press that he and a few friends were forming their own distribution company, United Artists (UA). His partners in the venture were Chaplin, Mary Pickford, and director D. W. Griffith. Fairbanks's announcement alarmed many studio executives, who saw it as proof that the stars were becoming too independent. As Richard Rowland, the head of Metro, put it, "The lunatics have taken over the asylum!"

But Mary Pickford was no lunatic. One of the shrewdest people in Hollywood, she knew that by forming their own corporation, she and her partners would enjoy complete artistic independence (a crucial factor, especially for Chaplin and Griffith). Pickford also knew the value of becoming one's own employer. By producing and distributing their own films, she and the others could keep all the profits for themselves.

The United Artists Corporation was founded in the spring of 1919. Fairbanks, Pickford, and Griffith began contributing films as quickly as they could, but upon his return from Europe in late 1921, Chaplin still had two pictures to deliver to First National. He completed them both in just under nine months.

The first, *Pay Day*, is considered one of Chaplin's less successful films. A simple comedy about a laborer who works at a construction site, it was the last two-reeler Chaplin ever made. In the future, he would concentrate all his efforts on feature- or near-feature-length productions.

In April 1922, he began to direct his final film for First

National. In *The Pilgrim*, an escaped convict (Charlie) steals a minister's outfit and flees by train to the small border town of Devil's Gulch, Texas. As it happens, the residents of Devil's Gulch are awaiting the arrival of a new minister and, to his surprise, Charlie finds himself in the awkward position of having to impersonate a parson. In one of the film's funniest scenes, he delivers a sermon on the Biblical story of David and Goliath, pantomiming both parts with consummate skill (after the "performance," he takes bows, blows kisses to the congregation, then returns for encores).

Upon its release in February 1923, *The Pilgrim* was criticized by some church authorities for poking fun at small-town puritanism. In one scene, for example, a minister leans over to reveal a whiskey bottle sticking out of his coat pocket. Sight gags such as this caused one Southern evangelical group to condemn the film as "an insult to the Gospel." In Pennsylvania, censors went so far as to ban the comedy altogether, claiming that it made the ministry look foolish.

With the completion of *The Pilgrim*, Chaplin was finally free to begin producing films for his own company, United Artists. Despite the popularity of such UA releases as *Pollyanna* (1920) and *The Three Musketeers* (1921), the corporation was steadily losing money. It was hoped that a full-length comedy featuring the Little Tramp might turn things around.

Chaplin, however, wasn't about to compromise his art for the sake of commercial success. After giving it much thought, he announced that his next film would be *A Woman of Paris*, a drama starring Edna Purviance and Adolphe Menjou. The comedian must have known that such a film would have limited appeal, but this did not concern him. He was growing tired of the character of the Little Tramp and felt it was time to explore other facets of his creativity. For once, Chaplin wanted to produce a serious "art" film.

Eight reels in length, *A Woman of Paris* was based in part on the life of Peggy Hopkins Joyce, a beautiful millionairess whom Chaplin had met the previous summer. Joyce's scandalous tales about her early life in Paris inspired Chaplin to write an original story about an innocent country girl named Marie St. Clair. After a misunderstanding with her boyfriend, Jean, she takes the train to Paris—a "magic city," a title reads, "where fortune is fickle and a woman gambles with life." There she becomes the mistress of Pierre Revel, a wealthy and cynical man. After many romantic complications, the story ends violently with the suicide of Marie's boyfriend, Jean, who has come to Paris to study art.

Chaplin spent ten months working on the film, which he subtitled "a drama of fate." From the start, he told the cast that he wanted the picture to be as realistic as possible. This worried Adolphe Menjou, who was playing the part of Pierre Revel. His method of acting was old-fashioned, and he knew it: "I had been schooled in the exaggerated gestures and reactions that were thought necessary to tell a story in pantomime."[10]

During the making of *A Woman of Paris*, Menjou had to forget everything he had been taught and adopt a style of acting that was much more sophisticated and subtle. Under no circumstances would Chaplin allow any of the actors to give an artificial or melodramatic performance. "Think the scene!" he kept telling them. "I don't care what you do with your hands or your feet. If you *think* the scene, it will get over." This was a new and unusual approach to film acting, and many sequences had to be shot over and over until the director was satisfied. The result, however, was well worth it. It was remarkable, said Menjou, how much information could be conveyed "with just a look, a gesture, a lifted eyebrow."

In September 1922, Pola Negri arrived in Hollywood to begin making pictures for Paramount. The twenty-four-year-old actress had fond memories of her days with Chaplin in Berlin and was eager to see her "jazz boy" again. The two actors met at a charity pageant at the Hollywood Bowl, where Chaplin was conducting the orchestra. "Chaarlee!" Negri cried in her Polish accent. "Why haven't I heard from you? Don't you realize I have come all the way from Germany to see you?"[11]

Chaplin knew this wasn't true, but he was flattered nevertheless. Soon he and Negri were dating, much to the delight of Hollywood gossips, who predicted a wedding in the near future. In January 1923, the two stars announced their engagement, but then, a mere five weeks later, the wedding was called off. "Now," Negri tearfully told the press, "I will live only for my work. As for the rest, the happy days are dead for me." Then, to everyone's surprise, the couple reunited, seemingly happier than ever.

The relationship, though, was doomed from the start. Chaplin, for his part, found all the publicity distasteful, while Negri complained that her lover was "too temperamental. . . . he dramatizes everything." After months of quarreling and making up, the pair formally separated in the summer of 1923. As usual, it was Negri who had the last word. "Mr. Chaplin," she told reporters, "should never marry. He has not any quality for matrimony. I am glad it is over."[12]

While Chaplin was producing *A Woman of Paris*, he purchased a six-and-a-half-acre lot in Beverly Hills, upon which he built a spacious, two-story home. In addition to a swimming pool, theater, and tennis court, the house contained a built-in steam room, where the comedian would usually head after a hard day's work. According to one source, the house was constructed by carpenters from the Chaplin Studio, who were used to building sets that could be quickly dismantled. Almost from the day Chaplin moved in, bits and pieces of his new home began to fall apart. Behind his back, friends called it "Breakaway House."

7

LITA GREY AND
THE GOLD RUSH

FEW FILMS OF THE SILENT ERA were as well received as *A Woman of Paris*, which opened in New York in October 1923. Nearly every critic hailed it as an extraordinary achievement. Said the *New York Herald Tribune*: "There is more real genius in Charles Chaplin's *A Woman of Paris* than in any picture I have ever seen." *Exceptional Photoplays* commended the drama for its "dignity and intelligence," while in England, the *Manchester Guardian* pronounced it "the greatest modern story" ever put on film.

A Woman of Paris was a bold and daring work, unlike anything Chaplin had done before. For this very reason, however, the public chose to stay away, and the box-office returns were extremely disappointing. In the United States, the film grossed less than $650,000 (*The Kid*, by contrast, had taken in $2.5 million). At this point, Chaplin realized he had no choice. If he wanted to maintain his popularity, his next film would have to be a comedy, one that featured the Little Tramp.

Coming up with a suitable story, however, proved troublesome. "For weeks," he said, "I strove, thought and brooded, trying to get an idea. . . . But nothing would come."[1] Then, one Sunday morning, he was looking at some photographs taken during the Alaskan gold rush. In one photo, a long line of prospectors mounted the Chilkoot Pass, a steep mountain separating them from the gold fields of the Klondike. In his mind, Chaplin could see the Tramp scaling the mountain, too, getting into all sorts of comedic trouble. Ideas began to come quickly, and by Monday morning he was busy laying the foundation for his next film, *The Gold Rush*.

Chaplin's crew spent the next few months researching the time period, scouting locations, building sets, and exchanging story ideas. Chaplin, meanwhile, had decided not to use Edna Purviance in the film. Sadly, Purviance had begun to drink on the job—not heavily, but enough to make her an unreliable performer. She could sense Chaplin's disappointment, which only served to undermine her confidence. After the failure of *A Woman of Paris*, it was announced to the press that Chaplin was seeking a new leading lady, and among those who showed up for an interview was a pretty teenager named Lillita McMurray.

Chaplin was already acquainted with the girl—she had appeared in two of his previous films, *The Kid* and *The Idle Class*. Since then, Lillita had matured considerably, but she was still young, only fifteen. Chaplin, however, was delighted with her screen test, and before anyone could change his mind, he signed Lillita to a $75 per week contract. He also persuaded the teenager to change her professional name. Henceforward, she would be known to the public as Lita Grey.

Chaplin began shooting *The Gold Rush* in February 1924. In the film, he played a "Lone Prospector" who, upon arriving in Alaska, befriends another gold seeker, Big Jim McKay (Mack Swain). Soon the two men are snowbound in their cabin. Gradually, starvation sets in. By Thanksgiving, the situation has become so desperate that they are forced to boil and eat one of Charlie's boots.

In a famous scene from The Gold Rush *(1925), the Little Tramp prepares to eat his boiled bootlaces. Many film critics and historians consider* The Gold Rush *to be Chaplin's masterpiece.*

While Big Jim waits to be served, Charlie pokes the steaming boot with a fork to see if it is done. Then, carefully, he separates the unappetizing, nail-studded sole from the upper, "meatier" part. Big Jim is repulsed by the idea of eating shoe leather, but Charlie is determined to keep an open mind. First, he takes a small bite; to his surprise, he discovers the sole is quite edible. So are the shoelaces, which he twirls around his fork like spaghetti. He even finds satisfaction in the nails, sucking them like meat-covered bones.

This "meal," however, does nothing to satisfy Big Jim's appetite. Driven mad from hunger, he imagines that Charlie is an oversized chicken and begins chasing him around the cabin, first with a knife, then with a gun.

Oddly enough, this amusing scene was inspired by the grim story of the Donner Party, a group of pioneers who became snowbound in the Sierra Nevada during the winter of 1846–47. When their food supply ran out, the starving pioneers had to resort to cannibalism to survive. The story of the Donner Party would appear to be an unlikely source for comedy but, as Chaplin once observed, tragedy and humor are closely allied. "Ridicule, I suppose, is an attitude of defiance: we must laugh in the face of our helplessness against the forces of nature—or go insane."[2]

The Gold Rush is one of Chaplin's funniest, most inventive films. It is also one of his most poignant. Midway through the story, the Little Tramp falls in love with Georgia, a spirited dance-hall girl. It's clear to the audience that Georgia cares nothing for Charlie; however, sensing his loneliness, she and her friends agree to dine with him on New Year's Eve, thus setting the stage for the film's most powerful sequence.

After buying presents and preparing an elaborate meal, Charlie sits down at the table to wait for his guests to arrive. The scene dissolves to the dinner party in progress. The young women are having a wonderful time and, to keep them entertained, Charlie announces that he will dance the "Oceana Roll." Selecting two forks, he spears them into a pair of bread rolls. Then, by manipulating the forks, he transforms the rolls into a pair of nimble feet, which hop, slide, shuffle, and high-kick their way across the tabletop. (When *The Gold Rush* premiered in Berlin, the "Dance of the Rolls" caused such a sensation that the projectionist had to rewind the film and run the scene again—to even greater applause.)

Delighted by his performance, Georgia kisses Charlie, causing him to faint. The scene dissolves to reveal the Little Tramp seated at the untouched table, fast asleep. Georgia, meanwhile, is seen at the Monte Carlo dance hall, ringing in the New Year with her pals. At midnight, she celebrates by firing off a revolver, awakening the Tramp in his cabin. With a heavy heart, he realizes the party was nothing but a dream. In a softly lit shot, he stands at the open door of the cabin, listening sadly to the distant strains of music coming from the dance hall. "For dramatic pathos," says Theodore Huff, "the New Year's Eve dinner sequence has seldom been surpassed in any medium."[3]

Lita Grey had been signed to play the role of Georgia, and during the early stages of shooting, Chaplin was extremely pleased with her performance. He was convinced that the teenager had a great deal of talent and, as filming progressed, he began to treat her as his protégée, taking her to premieres, to concerts, and to fancy restaurants. Then, unwisely, he took her home to seduce her.

Lita was not surprised, nor did she resist Chaplin's advances. From the moment she started work on *The Gold Rush*, she sensed that she and her director would eventually become lovers. It was no secret, she wrote, "that Charlie had a penchant for young girls. He approached them as projects, and indeed, cared for some of them. He liked to cultivate them, to gain their trust, . . . and to create them as scrupulously as he created a motion picture."[4]

Because Lita was only sixteen and therefore a minor, she and Chaplin had to keep their relationship a secret,

As her mother and Charlie look on, Lita Grey signs a contract to become Chaplin's leading lady in The Gold Rush. *An unplanned pregnancy prevented her from finishing the picture.*

especially from Lillian Spicer, Lita's strong-willed mother. Said Lita: "Working out elaborate schemes to escape Mama's watchful eye became a game between Charlie and me, and we grew adept at it."[5]

In September 1924, Lita's happiness came to an abrupt end when she discovered that she was pregnant. Her mother was extremely upset and, meeting privately with Chaplin, she demanded that he marry Lita as quickly as possible. At first, the comedian fiercely denied being the father of Lita's baby; later, in a somewhat calmer mood, he offered to pay for an abortion. The longer Chaplin stalled, the angrier Lillian became. Finally, she issued an ultimatum: he would either marry Lita or face an immediate lawsuit. The choice, she said, was up to him.

A few weeks later, on November 26, Chaplin married Lita in the small town of Empalme, near Guaymas, in northern Mexico. He had sought out this remote spot to avoid publicity, but the marriage could not be kept a secret for long. Nor could Lita's pregnancy, which made it impossible for her to continue her work in *The Gold Rush.* One month after the wedding, Chaplin informed the press that he had selected a pretty eighteen-year-old named Georgia Hale as his new leading lady. At the same time, to discourage reporters from asking about Lita, he announced that his wife was feeling ill and could not be interviewed. Lita, in fact, would be kept hidden from the public eye for the duration of her pregnancy.

As soon as Georgia Hale could be fitted for costumes, Chaplin resumed work on *The Gold Rush,* finishing the picture in May 1925. By that time, Lita had been quietly moved to a rented house in the area to await the arrival of the baby. Shortly after dawn on May 4, Chaplin received a telephone call informing him that his wife had gone into premature labor. The following day, after a long and difficult delivery, Lita gave birth to a son, whom she named Charles, Jr. Ever since the shotgun wedding in Mexico, Chaplin's attitude toward his wife had been cold and resentful. Now, to Lita's astonishment, his behavior changed dramatically. He became a loving and considerate husband, she said, one who spent his time "seeing that my every need and desire were filled and basking in the wonder of his son."[6]

Though Chaplin's heart was softening, he had very little time to spend with his family. He and his staff were putting in long hours at the studio, editing *The Gold Rush*. The film received its world premiere at Grauman's Egyptian Theatre in Hollywood on the evening of June 26, 1925. Despite the enthusiasm with which it was received, Chaplin was not entirely satisfied with the film. Later that week, he returned to the studio to make some additional cuts. He also hired a composer to prepare a musical score for the picture.

In late July, accompanied by his Japanese manservant, Chaplin traveled to New York to attend the East Coast premiere. Physically and emotionally, he felt exhausted. At his New York hotel, he found himself weeping for no apparent reason. Then he began to have respiratory problems. By the night of August 11, he had convinced himself that he was dying. In a panic, he called not for a doctor but for his lawyer. He wanted to make sure that his will was in satisfactory order.

Clearly, Chaplin was on the verge of a nervous breakdown. And yet, somehow he managed to pull himself together in time for the August 16 premiere of *The Gold Rush*. The event, held at the Mark Strand Theater, was a tremendous success, and the subsequent reviews were among the strongest of Chaplin's career. "*The Gold Rush* is the funniest film I have ever seen," said St. John Ervine in *The Living Age*. "It is probably the funniest film that anyone has ever seen." The *New York Times* called it "by all means Chaplin's supreme effort," while *Variety* predicted that it would create "a veritable riot at theater box offices." Eventually taking in $4 million, *The Gold Rush* was one of the most successful films of the 1920s. Nor would its critical luster fade: more than thirty years later, an international jury selected it as the second greatest film ever made (*The Battleship Potemkin*, a silent drama by Russian filmmaker Sergei Eisenstein, came in first).

Chaplin was by no means the only comedian producing quality work during this period. Buster Keaton, Harry Langdon, and Harold Lloyd were all big box-office draws. Keaton was as good an acrobat as Chaplin, and Lloyd's films were memorable for their hair-raising scenes of suspense. But when filmgoers spoke of the Little Tramp, it was with a sense of genuine affection. As far as the critics were concerned, Chaplin's artistry was beyond reproach; according to one writer, he was the only silent film comedian "who got any serious critical attention at the time."

Following the mid-August premiere, Chaplin lingered in New York for another six weeks—an indication, perhaps, that he and his wife were not getting along. Then, in early October, Lita informed her husband that she was pregnant again.

The news did not please Chaplin. By the time he had returned to Los Angeles, he had worked himself into a fury. For several days, he subjected Lita to a steady stream of verbal abuse. Then, suddenly, he became distant and withdrawn. Lita was deeply confused by her husband's erratic behavior; increasingly, she began to realize that their marriage was doomed.

During this unhappy period, Chaplin's coworkers must have feared that his creativity would suffer. Fortunately, this did not happen. In January 1926, Chaplin began shooting *The Circus*, one of his most entertaining comedies. The film opens brightly with an extended chase sequence. Mistaken for a pickpocket at a carnival, the Little Tramp is being pursued by a policeman. To escape, he dashes into a circus tent, where his unintentional antics are a hit with the audience. Impressed, the owner of the circus (Allan Garcia) asks him to come back for a tryout the following day.

Unfortunately, the audition is a disaster: Charlie, it seems, has no natural gift for comedy. Nevertheless, he is hired as a property man and general assistant, a setup that allows Chaplin to indulge himself in numerous sight gags (when Charlie is asked, for instance, to blow a pill down the throat of a sick horse, the horse blows first, lodging the huge pill in Charlie's throat).

In time, quite by accident, Charlie becomes the "star clown" of the circus. Meanwhile, he has fallen in love with the circus owner's stepdaughter, a pretty bareback rider (Merna Kennedy). The girl is fond of Charlie, but her heart belongs to Rex, a handsome tightrope walker. To impress the bareback rider and to build his self-esteem, the Tramp spends many hours teaching himself to walk the tightrope. In the film's most thrilling sequence, he is suddenly called upon to replace Rex on the high wire. Believing that his safety halter is securely attached, Charlie begins the act with complete confidence—only to realize, halfway across the wire, that the halter has come loose. Before he can return to the platform, he is set upon by a group of monkeys, who pull down his trousers and generally threaten to upset his balance.

As might be expected, *The Circus* contains a number of excellent comedy routines. Chaplin clearly loved the world of the big top; the look and atmosphere of the film are wonderfully authentic. The story, however, is not particularly well written, and some of the scenes involving the bareback rider and her abusive stepfather are unnecessarily melodramatic. Though Chaplin would later receive a special Academy Award for writing and directing *The Circus*, he could never shake the feeling that the film was something of a disappointment.[7]

The production, moreover, was beset by disasters, large and small. A rainstorm damaged the circus tent; scratches were discovered on the film, forcing Chaplin to reshoot a number of scenes; then, one night, a mysterious fire broke out, completely destroying the set. Nobody was injured, but Chaplin was heartbroken by the extent of the damage.

His marriage, meanwhile, continued to unravel. In March 1926, Lita gave birth to a son named Sydney. The baby's arrival did nothing to improve Chaplin's attitude toward his wife. By now, he was convinced that he'd been tricked into marrying Lita and that she and her mother were planning to ruin him financially. Ugly words were exchanged between husband and wife; there were times, according to Lita, when Chaplin's behavior bordered on the psychotic. "The subject of divorce," she said, "[became] a matter of fanaticism with him, and he would come to me or summon me and rant about nothing else."[8]

Finally, Lita could stand it no longer. One day, while Chaplin was at the studio, she packed her bags, collected the children, and moved out. A few weeks later, in January 1927, her lawyers filed a divorce complaint. Fifty-two pages in length, it was an astonishing and disturbing document. In it, Lita claimed that Chaplin had subjected her to "cruel and inhuman treatment"; that he had been unfaithful to her on numerous occasions; that his sexual desires were "abnormal . . . indecent and immoral"; and that during their honeymoon, on the train back from Mexico, he had actually suggested she commit suicide.

Lita later admitted that some of the charges in the complaint had been deliberately distorted for shock value. At the time, however, the document served its purpose, catapulting the details of Chaplin's private life onto the front page of every newspaper in the country.

Deeply distraught, the comedian halted production of *The Circus* and fled to New York, where the accumulated stress caused him to suffer a nervous breakdown. His lawyer encouraged him to settle with Lita quickly, but Chaplin was determined to fight his wife every step of the way. In June, he filed his own complaint, accusing Lita of being a heavy drinker, a neglectful mother, and an unfaithful wife. By that time, however, the public had already sided against him, especially after the papers reported that the Chaplin babies were going hungry because their father refused to pay for their milk. It was an absurd charge, but Lita and her lawyers did nothing to refute it.

The anguish of the divorce took a heavy toll on Chaplin physically. One morning, he awoke to discover that his graying hair had turned completely white. "I was shocked, profoundly shocked," said one of his employees. "My God, if ever anybody wanted proof of what Charlie had been through, there it was."[9]

After dragging out the case as long as he could, Chaplin conceded defeat. In August 1927, in a Los Angeles courtroom, Lita was awarded $625,000, a record sum at the time. She was also given custody of her sons, Charles and Sydney, each of whom received $100,000 in the form of a trust fund. Though embittered by the judge's ruling, Chaplin was relieved to have the case settled once and for all.

In early September, he returned to the studio to resume work on *The Circus*. He had nearly completed the picture when another event occurred that would have a profound impact on his life and career. On October 6, 1927, Warner Brothers premiered its first full-length talking picture, *The Jazz Singer*, starring Al Jolson. Featuring a handful of songs and snippets of spoken dialogue, *The Jazz Singer* created a sensation throughout America. Overnight, it seemed, movie theaters were being wired for sound and all the studios were scrambling to take advantage of the new medium.

Many people in Hollywood were alarmed by the advent of the "talkies." One was Joseph Schenck, the president of United Artists, who predicted that sound pictures would quickly fade from the scene. Schenck was a good businessman, but he was dead wrong about the popularity of the talkies. Within a year and a half of the release of *The Jazz Singer*, silent pictures had become a thing of the past.

8

THE BEAUTY OF SILENCE

TALKING PICTURES WERE nothing new. Some historians believe that sound and film were successfully synchronized as early as 1889. The methods of playback, however, were extremely crude, and it was not until the fall of 1927 that talking pictures began to catch on. For a while, silent films continued to do good business; *The Circus*, for instance, was a big hit, taking in more than $3 million. But by late 1928, the truth could no longer be avoided: silent pictures were on their way out.

Like many others in the industry, Charlie Chaplin viewed the talkies with disdain. "They are spoiling the oldest art in the world," he maintained, "the art of pantomime. They are ruining the great beauty of silence."[1] He also suspected that talking pictures would be more difficult to market in foreign countries (his most important source of revenue). Pantomime, after all, was an international language; English was not.

Chaplin's biggest worry, however, had to do with the fate of the Little Tramp. Charlie was fundamentally a silent character. To put words into his mouth would inevitably strip him of some of his appeal and make him less universal.

Comedians Harold Lloyd and Buster Keaton faced the same dilemma: could they—should they—adapt? To the regret of their fans, all three would eventually be forced to abandon silent comedy. According to one writer, Tom Dardis, the introduction of sound "literally meant the death of the art of Chaplin, Lloyd, and Keaton. . . . In none of their sound films did these three men ever rise to the heights they reached in the silent era. Their art had nothing to do with words: all three lost their unique magic the moment they opened their mouths."[2]

Chaplin held out the longest. Shortly after completing *The Circus*, he began to write the scenario for *City Lights*, one of his most beautiful and most successful silent pictures. At first, he wanted to tell the story of a clown who loses his sight in an accident, then attempts to hide his disability from his nervous, sickly daughter. But that plot, Chaplin decided, was "too 'icky.'" Nevertheless, he was intrigued by the theme of blindness, and over the next several months he began to craft a simple but dramatic story about a blind flower girl and her unusual relationship with a homeless tramp.

The two characters meet in a memorable way. While crossing the street, the Tramp nimbly avoids a policeman by stepping into the back of a parked limousine, then exiting from the other side. Hearing a car door open, the flower girl assumes that a wealthy gentleman has alighted. "Flower, sir?" she inquires. The Tramp spends his last coin to buy a flower, which he accidentally knocks from the girl's hand. As he watches her grope about, trying to find it, it slowly dawns on him that the flower girl cannot see. By the time he leaves the stand, he has fallen in love with her beauty and unaffected charm.

That evening, at the river's edge, Charlie comes upon an unhappy millionaire (Harry Myers) who is about to commit suicide by drowning himself. Charlie manages to save the man, who gratefully takes him back to his mansion, plies him with drink, then takes him out for a wild evening on the town. It is the beginning of a close but curious relationship. Whenever the millionaire is drunk, he loves to have Charlie around, but when sober he has no recollection of his "best friend" and throws him out of the house. The millionaire is unpredictable, but he is also extremely generous. Happily, this allows Charlie to keep up the pretense with the flower girl that he is a wealthy man.

Midway through the film, the Tramp learns that the girl's sight can be restored if she goes to Vienna for an operation. Unable to raise enough to pay for her boat passage himself, he explains the situation to the millionaire, who drunkenly gives him the money he needs. The minute he sobers up, however, the tycoon is convinced he has been robbed. Charlie has just enough time to pass on the money to the flower girl before he is arrested and thrown into jail.

Several months later, the Tramp is released from prison, a broken man. As he trudges sadly down the street, the flower girl, now cured, catches sight of him through the window of her shop. Never having seen the Tramp before, she has no idea who he is, but out of pity she offers him a coin and a flower. Embarrassed, Charlie tries to hurry away, but the girl is insistent. Reaching out, she takes his hand—and at that moment recognizes her benefactor by touch.

"You?" she asks in disbelief. Charlie nods. As the girl's eyes begin to fill with tears, the Tramp continues to look at her, fearful, optimistic, a finger pressed nervously to his lips. Gradually, the film fades out.

It is an ambiguous ending—will the girl accept Charlie or reject him?—and therein lies its emotional power. The final scene of *City Lights*, says critic James Agee, "is enough to shrivel the heart. . . . It is the greatest piece of acting and the highest moment in movies."[3]

Like *The Circus, City Lights* was a troubled production, one that suffered numerous delays and setbacks. An ongoing source of frustration was Virginia Cherrill, the young woman who played the flower girl. A socialite from Chicago, Cherrill had no previous acting experience, and it was only with the greatest difficulty that Chaplin was able to extract from her the performance he desired. Another serious setback occurred in October 1929, when the New York Stock Exchange collapsed. Chaplin himself was not badly affected by the crash, but countless Americans were. Though very few realized it at the time, it was the beginning of a worldwide economic depression.

By the time Chaplin finished *City Lights* in late 1930, the entire motion picture industry had converted to sound. Despite his dislike of the talkies, Chaplin had tentatively begun to experiment with the microphone. While *City Lights* contained no spoken dialogue, it included a number of amusing sound effects, as well as a synchronized musical score, much of which Chaplin composed himself. Though he could not read music, he was a gifted musician, and he thoroughly enjoyed the task of preparing the score for his new picture, which he subtitled "a comedy romance in pantomime."

The world premiere of *City Lights* was held in Los Angeles on January 30, 1931. That afternoon, a large and excited crowd began to gather outside the theater to witness the arrival of such celebrities as Cecil B. De Mille, Gloria Swanson, John Barrymore, and guest of honor Albert Einstein. To Chaplin's relief, the premiere was a great success, as was the New York opening, held one week later. Then, on February 9, a photo of the Little Tramp appeared on the cover of *Time* magazine. All this hoopla convinced the public that *City Lights* was a must-see. The film went on to become one of the biggest hits of 1931, taking in more than $5 million worldwide. According to one writer, this was perhaps "an indirect comment on the quality of talking pictures people had been subjected to in

Charlie escorts physicist Albert Einstein (left) and Elsa Einstein (right) to the Los Angeles premiere of City Lights *(1931).*

the past four years. It may be that *City Lights* reminded them of something valuable they had lost."[4]

In February 1931, Chaplin sailed to England to attend the film's London premiere. Shortly thereafter, he embarked on a lengthy European tour, traveling first to Berlin, then to Vienna, where he was greeted by a large and tumultuous crowd. He found Venice depressing (it was the off-season), but his spirits were revived in Paris, where he was made a Chevalier of the Legion of Honor. Then, heading to the south of France, he spent time with his brother, Sydney, who had retired after a successful Hollywood career, both as a comedian and as his brother's business agent.

For nearly a year, Chaplin drifted from one city to another, trying to keep himself amused. As he later confessed in his autobiography, he was terrified by the thought of returning to Hollywood, a place that no longer had much use for a silent film comedian. "Occasionally," he said, "I mused over the possibility of making a sound film, but the thought sickened me, for I realized I could never achieve the excellence of my silent pictures."[5]

In this fretful state, Chaplin continued to wander: to Algiers, to Spain, then to Switzerland, where he spent the winter with his friend Douglas Fairbanks. Finally, in March 1932, Chaplin and his brother embarked for the Far East, where they visited Ceylon, Singapore, and the island of Bali, a spot they found particularly enchanting. The final stop on the world tour was Japan, where, among other treats, Chaplin enjoyed the spectacle of Kabuki theater.

The comedian finally returned to Los Angeles in June 1932. Instead of reopening his studio, he spent the next seven months writing a detailed account of his travels for a popular women's magazine.[6] He was still feeling confused and depressed about his career. "Without doubt silent pictures were finished," he said, "and I did not feel like combatting the talkies." Deeply discouraged, he considered retiring from pictures, selling his property, and moving to China.

Then, to his surprise, Chaplin found a reason to stay. In the summer of 1932, he was introduced to a twenty-one-year-old actress named Paulette Goddard. Intelligent, ambitious, and extremely pretty, Paulette worked as a bit player at the Hal Roach studio. That summer, she and Chaplin spent a great deal of time together, driving up the coast or taking leisurely boat trips to nearby Catalina Island. Inevitably, gossip columnists began to hint that the two were engaged, but Paulette denied it, explaining that she and the director were simply good friends.

One of the things that Chaplin liked best about Paulette was her lively sense of humor. She also projected a certain vivaciousness that, as a director, he found immensely appealing. "[She] struck me," he said, "as being somewhat of a *gamine*," a child of the streets. "This would be a wonderful quality . . . to get on the screen."[7] Gradually, Chaplin began to take control of Paulette's career. He encouraged her, for instance, to take singing and dancing lessons; he also instructed her to change the color of her hair, from platinum blonde to brunette. Then, with her permission, he bought up her Hal Roach contract—a clear sign that he intended to make her his next leading lady.

Meanwhile, he was thinking about his next film project. A number of possibilities came to mind, only to be quickly discarded. Then, by chance, Chaplin recalled a conversation he had had with a young newspaper reporter. It concerned the big car factories in Detroit, where the workers were so stressed by the conveyor-belt system of production that many were suffering from nervous collapse. Just as Chaplin had visualized the Tramp scaling the Chilkoot Pass, he could now easily imagine the little fellow trying to keep up with the hectic pace of a conveyor belt. From this germ of an idea, Chaplin began to write the story for his next comedy, *Modern Times*.

Early on, he was faced with a difficult decision. Should it be a silent film or a talkie? After giving it great thought, Chaplin decided to stick to pantomime, the style of acting he knew best. Financially, he knew he was taking a tremendous risk, but as an artist he was not ready to give up the silent medium. According to his son, Charles, Jr., "Everyone in Hollywood thought my father was crazy. . . . People began to think of him . . . [as] a has-been, unable to adjust himself to the new techniques. He was finished in pictures—you heard that all over town."[8]

Chaplin and his staff spent the next two years preparing the story for *Modern Times*, which went into production in October 1934. The first (and most famous) part of the film takes place at the Electro Steel Company, where Charlie has a nerve-racking job, tightening nuts onto double bolts as they move along a never-ending conveyer belt. When he realizes he's missed a nut, he attempts to chase it down the assembly line, ultimately getting himself caught inside the gears of a great machine.

The owner of the factory is a tyrant, constantly barking orders through a loudspeaker. In one of the film's funniest scenes, he selects Charlie to demonstrate an automatic feeding machine, one that will allow employees to eat and work at the same time (thus eliminating the lunch break). At first, the demonstration goes well; then, without warning, a short circuit causes everything to speed up. Hot soup is poured into Charlie's lap; a revolving cob of corn grinds furiously against his teeth; steel bolts are pushed into his mouth; for dessert, a piece of pie is hurled into his face.

At last, the machine self-destructs, and Charlie is sent back to his nut-tightening job, the repetitive nature of which causes him to go crazy. In his dementia, he dances like a faun through the factory, squirting oil on his coworkers and trying to tighten anything that looks like a nut. An ambulance is summoned and, still clutching his oil can, Charlie is taken away to the hospital for a much-needed rest.

"Cured of a nervous breakdown," a title reads, "but without a job," the Little Tramp attempts to start life anew.

The Little Tramp gets caught up in his work in this publicity shot from Modern Times *(1936).*

On the street, he happens to see a red warning flag fall off the bed of a passing truck. Helpfully, he picks up the flag and waves it, trying to get the driver's attention. At that moment, a group of unemployed men march around the corner. Spotting the red flag (a symbol of Communism), they automatically fall in behind their "leader." The police arrive on the scene and, to Charlie's bewilderment, he is arrested as a Communist agitator.

Later, when he is a free man again, Charlie meets up with a teenage gamine (Paulette Goddard). A scrappy girl, she is fleeing from the juvenile authorities, who plan to take her to the county orphanage. The rest of the film chronicles her various adventures with Charlie, as the two try to cope with all the pressures and anxieties of "modern times."

Talented as well as pretty, the gamine eventually finds work as a dancer at a café. She, in turn, persuades the manager to hire Charlie as a waiter. That night, he is ordered to sing a song for the customers. To help Charlie remember the lyrics, the gamine writes them on the cuff of his sleeve. The moment the music begins, however, his cuff flies off, and he is forced to improvise by singing in a gibberish language. This was the first and only time Chaplin allowed the public to hear the Little Tramp's voice. Yet, by having him speak nonsensical words, Chaplin managed to retain to the very end the character's universal appeal.

At the café that same evening, the gamine is apprehended by the juvenile authorities. She and the Tramp manage to escape, but at the cost of losing their jobs. The next morning, alongside a deserted road, the gamine begins to weep bitterly. Charlie tries to lift her spirits by telling her to "buck up. Never say die. We'll get along!" With Charlie's help, the gamine rediscovers her courage. The film closes with one of Chaplin's most celebrated shots: arm in arm, the gamine and the Tramp take to the road, heading "toward the sun that promises a brighter tomorrow."

After two successful previews, *Modern Times* opened in New York City on February 5, 1936. The film did well at the box office, but the reviews were mixed. Some critics complained that it was too serious for a comedy. Others (political leftists in particular) felt that *Modern Times* was *too* lighthearted, that Chaplin should have taken a more satiric jab at capitalism. The film, grumbled one critic, "[is] neither fish, flesh, nor good red propaganda."

To some extent, *Modern Times* was a victim of depression-era mentality. During this stressful period, when millions of people were out of work, American artists were expected to show their sympathy for the problems of the poor. In Hollywood, for instance, directors were encour-

Paulette Goddard, pictured here in a 1936 publicity shot, starred as the gamine in Modern Times. *She and Charlie were secretly married in 1936; they separated in 1940.*

aged to make films that treated the depression in a realistic way. It also became commonplace for writers and filmmakers to show their commitment to some political philosophy. Chaplin was willing to do this, but only to a point. As he explained to the press, he was a comedian, not a propagandist: "To entertain is my first consideration. . . . I have no political aims whatsoever as an actor."[9]

One person who agreed with his position was Kate Cameron, the critic for the *New York Daily News*. "It had been hinted," she wrote, "that Chaplin had gone serious on us and that he had . . . [an important message] to deliver to the world in *Modern Times*. No such thing has happened, thank goodness. . . . There is nothing of real significance in Chaplin's work except his earnest desire, and his great ability, to entertain."[10]

Two weeks after the premiere of *Modern Times*, Chaplin sailed to Hawaii, then continued on to the Orient. He was accompanied by Paulette; her mother, Alta; and Frank Yonamori, his Japanese manservant. During the three-and-a-half-month voyage, Chaplin and Paulette were married aboard the ship. Upon their return to California, however, they would not confirm to the press that a wedding had taken place. Nor would they deny it. It was an odd, even reckless, game the Chaplins would continue to play with the public for the next four years.

9
PLAYING
THE VILLAIN

FINANCIALLY, *MODERN TIMES* was not as successful as *City Lights.* In the United States, the film earned only $1.4 million—a substantial amount in 1936, but a disappointment to Chaplin, who had hoped for a box-office smash. The following year, in September 1937, he made a startling announcement to the press: after considering the matter carefully, he had decided to abandon both the character of the Little Tramp and the medium of silent comedy. Ten years after the introduction of sound, he was finally ready to make his first talkie.

While acknowledging that the Tramp would be missed, most journalists felt that Chaplin was making the right decision. (In any case, said the *New York Times*, it was useless for anyone "to pretend that the sound revolution had passed over his head leaving him as firmly enthroned as ever.")[1]

Chaplin, meanwhile, was actively searching for his next film project. Among the many scripts under consideration, two seemed especially promising: *Regency*, an adaptation of a novel by D. L. Murray; and *Stowaway*, a love story Chaplin had written during his recent voyage to the Far East. He knew that his wife, Paulette, was anxious to make another film, and it frustrated them both that his creativity could not be hurried along.

The search was still under way when Chaplin met with British producer Alexander Korda, who suggested that he make a comedy about Adolf Hitler, the chancellor of Germany. The idea was not as perverse as it sounded. Ever since Hitler's ascent to power, people throughout the world had commented on his striking resemblance to the Little Tramp. The plot, Korda went on to say, might involve a case of mistaken identity, with the Tramp impersonating Hitler. Though Chaplin was intrigued by the concept, he chose not to pursue it. The idea, he said, was too grim for a comedy.

A few months later, in March 1938, German troops occupied Austria, an act of political aggression that shocked the world. At the time, Chaplin was in Pebble Beach, California, revising his *Stowaway* script. He tried to concentrate on his work, but he couldn't stop thinking about Hitler and the Nazi Party. The more Chaplin studied the political situation, the more convinced he became that Europe was on the brink of another war.

In Pebble Beach, he reconsidered Korda's suggestion, this time from a fresh perspective. As an artist, Chaplin knew that his films had the power to move people; as a humanitarian, he believed that Hitler had to be stopped. It was inevitable, perhaps, that his hatred for the Nazis would merge with his eagerness to make another film. By the time Chaplin returned to Hollywood that summer, he had begun to write the script for *The Great Dictator*, his first talking picture. The task would occupy him for more than a year.

In his autobiography, Chaplin admitted that had he known of "the actual horrors of the German concentration camps, I could not have made *The Great Dictator*; I could not have made fun of the homicidal insanity of the Nazis."[2] At the time, however, he believed he was doing the right thing. Chaplin sensed that if he could turn Hitler into the laughingstock of Europe, then a second world war might be averted. This, of course, did not happen, but his sincerity of purpose cannot be doubted.

Chaplin had just finished his script when, on September 1, 1939, Hitler's troops invaded Poland. Two days later, England and France declared war on Germany. At this early stage of the conflict, less than 10 percent of American citizens believed that the Germans would be victorious; nevertheless, for political reasons President Franklin D. Roosevelt was reluctant to speak out against Hitler. For the next fifteen months, in fact, the United States would declare itself neutral, refusing to get involved in the war in Europe.

In early September, Chaplin began to receive urgent telegrams from officials at United Artists, encouraging him to abandon his Hitler comedy—such a picture, they feared, could never be shown in the United States. "But I was determined to make [*The Great Dictator*]," said Chaplin, "even if I had to hire halls myself to show it."

Production began on September 9, one week after the outbreak of the war. In the film, Chaplin played two characters who look remarkably alike: Adenoid Hynkel, the dictator of Tomania, and one of his subjects, a barber who lives in the Jewish ghetto of a Tomanian city. Hynkel is first seen delivering a vigorous speech at a political rally. After denouncing such principles as liberty and free speech ("Libertad shtunk!"), he turns his anger upon the Jews, whom he considers enemies of the state. So strong is Hynkel's fury, so wild his gestures, that his speech becomes wholly unintelligible. Later, one of his comrades, Garbitsch, advises him to step up attacks on the Jewish people. "Perhaps you're right," Hynkel agrees. "Things have been quiet in the ghetto lately."

Tomanian storm troopers begin a new wave of persecution. One of their first victims is the barber, a World War I veteran who has just been released from the hospital after suffering from amnesia for twenty years; as a result,

In The Great Dictator *(1940), Charlie lampooned fascism, playing a dual role as a Jewish barber and a caricature of Adolf Hitler. It was Chaplin's first talking picture.*

he does not understand who the soldiers are and why they are painting the word "Jew" on his window. Another resident of the ghetto is a feisty young woman named Hannah (Paulette Goddard), who believes that the Jews must do everything they can to resist the storm troopers. "We can't fight [individually]," she tells the barber, "but we can lick 'em together."

Dissatisfied with his rate of progress, Hynkel decides to prove his political strength by invading the neighboring country of Austerlich. In the film's strangest and most beautiful scene, the dictator is standing alone in his office. Gently, he begins to toss a large, inflatable globe into the air like a balloon. Dreaming of world conquest, he twirls the globe; bumps it with his head; dances with it; then, swooning, clutches the world to his chest. The balloon pops and Hynkel throws himself onto his desk, sobbing.

In order to finance his Austerlich campaign, Hynkel must borrow a large sum of money from Epstein, a Jewish financier. When Epstein refuses to make the loan, Hynkel takes revenge by ordering a full-scale attack on the Jewish ghetto. In the ensuing raid, the barber is arrested and taken away to a concentration camp. To save herself, Hannah flees to Austerlich. Shortly thereafter, Hynkel's soldiers begin their invasion.

Toward the end of the film, the barber escapes from the concentration camp. It is at this point that the mix-up of identity occurs. Hynkel, temporarily out of uniform, is mistaken for the barber and "returned" to prison. The barber, meanwhile, who is wearing a stolen army uniform, is astonished when Tomanian troopers on the road salute him as Hynkel. At once, he is driven to the defeated capital of Austerlich, where he is scheduled to deliver a victory speech over the radio.

After making an address of his own, Garbitsch introduces Hynkel as "the future Emperor of the World!" Apprehensively, the little barber approaches the bank of microphones. Aware that millions are listening to the broadcast, the barber quietly says that he does not wish to be an emperor: "That's not my business. I don't want to rule or conquer anyone. I should like to help everyone, if possible—Jew, Gentile, black men, white."

As the speech continues, the barber encourages his listeners not to despair: "The way of life can be free and beautiful, but we have lost the way. . . . Our knowledge has made us cynical. . . . We think too much and feel too little. . . . More than cleverness, we need kindness and gentleness. Without these qualities, life will be violent and all will be lost."

With rising passion, the barber reminds everyone that "dictators die, and the power they took from the people will return to the people. . . . Let us fight," he cries, "to do away with greed, with hate and intolerance. . . . Soldiers, in the name of democracy, let us *unite!*"[3] The film ends with a beautiful shot of Hannah listening to the speech. Tears glistening in her eyes, she dreams of a brighter and more hopeful future for all the people of the world.

Due to its topical subject matter, *The Great Dictator* was one of the most controversial, eagerly anticipated films of its day. Accompanied by a tremendous amount of publicity, the film opened at two theaters in New York on October 15, 1940. Bosley Crowther, the critic for the *New York Times*, pronounced it "a superlative accomplishment by a great and true artist . . . unquestionably the most significant—if not the most entertaining—film that Chaplin has ever made."[4]

The majority of reviewers were less enthusiastic. The film, in their opinion, was a peculiar mix of comedy, drama, and political propaganda. To Chaplin's dismay, the closing speech was torn apart by the critics, who called it naive and embarrassing, "completely out of key with all that has preceded it." The *New York Sun* went so far as to label the film "a great disappointment."

Fortunately, the public did not agree. To the astonishment of everyone at United Artists, *The Great Dictator* went on to earn more than $5 million worldwide; according to

Chaplin, it was "the biggest grosser of all my pictures up to that time." The film later received five Academy Award nominations, including Best Picture, Best Actor, and Best Original Screenplay.

By 1940, most silent film stars had long since faded from the scene. Mary Pickford, for example, hadn't made a picture in years. Neither had Clara Bow or Lillian Gish or Norma Talmadge. Jackie Coogan was a has-been; so were directors Mack Sennett and D. W. Griffith. Gloria Swanson and Buster Keaton were still working, but they were no longer considered box-office attractions. Chaplin's career, on the other hand, appeared to be flourishing. His inspired performance in *The Great Dictator* had proved to the public that his genius was undimmed. At the age of fifty-one, Chaplin was still a vibrant artist, capable of adapting himself to changing times.

It was during this same period, in late 1940, that he and Paulette decided to separate. Though Chaplin was unable to pinpoint the cause of their troubles, it is likely that his obsessive working habits were partly to blame. "I am a very hard person to live with," he once admitted. "Every artist must be. . . . When I am working, I withdraw absolutely from those I love. I have no energy, no love to give them."[5] After a period of separation, Paulette traveled to Mexico, where she obtained a divorce on the grounds of mutual incompatibility.

In January 1941, Chaplin was asked to take part in the festivities surrounding the third inauguration of President Franklin D. Roosevelt. On the evening of January 19, before a large crowd in the nation's capital, Chaplin recited the final speech from *The Great Dictator*. According to his son Charles, Jr., the tremendous ovation his father received that evening "might be called the pinnacle of his public success in [America]. From then on the path led downward by subtle degrees until it ended in his self-imposed exile."[6]

Later that year, Chaplin was introduced to an attractive twenty-two-year-old named Joan Barry. An aspiring actress from New York, she had come to Los Angeles to break into the movies. A day or two after meeting Chaplin, she telephoned him, suggesting that he take her out that evening. According to the director, Barry was a persistent woman who wouldn't take no for an answer. "Thus," he said, "she achieved her object and I began to see her often." The relationship, sadly, was to have disastrous consequences.

In June 1941, around the time Chaplin met Barry, Germany invaded the Soviet Union. Hitler's troops advanced rapidly toward Moscow; by November, the Nazis had overrun all of southern Russia. Because the United States and Russia were allies, many Americans felt that President Roosevelt should respond by sending troops to western Europe. By opening a second front, the argument ran, Hitler would be forced to split his army, thereby ensuring a swift victory for the Allied nations. For good reason, however, the U.S. government was reluctant to adopt such a plan. It was felt that the American forces were not yet strong enough to win a war against Germany. For the time being, the Soviets would have to fend for themselves.

Like many people, Chaplin was frustrated by this "wait and see" attitude. The Russians, he maintained, "are in desperate need of help. They are pleading for a second front." Therefore, when the comedian was asked in May 1942 to speak in San Francisco on behalf of the Russians, he did not hesitate to accept.

Nearly ten thousand Bay Area citizens attended the Russian War Relief rally. Chaplin had originally planned to speak for only a few minutes; carried away by his own enthusiasm, he ended up speaking for forty. "I am not a Communist," he told the crowd. "I am a human being, and I think I know the reactions of human beings. The Communists are no different from anyone else; whether they lose an arm or a leg, they suffer as all of us do, and die as all of us die."[7] Chaplin finished his speech by urging every person in the hall to send a telegram to President

Roosevelt: "Let's hope that by tomorrow he will receive ten thousand requests for a second front!"

In the months to come, Chaplin would make six additional speeches on behalf of Russian War Relief. In October, for instance, he appeared at New York's Carnegie Hall, where he addressed the crowd as comrades: "Yes, I mean comrades. When one sees the magnificent fight the Russian people are putting up, it is a pleasure and a privilege to use the word 'comrade.'"[8] After the war, Chaplin would be severely criticized for his sympathetic remarks concerning the Communists. At the time, however, his speeches aroused no particular controversy; according to one biographer, the actor's views concerning Russia were "more or less in line with the policies of the day."

By mid-1942, Chaplin's relationship with Joan Barry had run its course. In its early stages, the affair had gone smoothly. "Then," according to Chaplin, "strange and eerie things began to happen. Barry began driving up in her Cadillac at all hours of the night, very drunk." On one occasion, she wrecked her car in the driveway; another time, when the actor refused to come to the door, Barry, in a fury, began smashing in the windows. "Overnight," Chaplin said, "my existence became a nightmare."

In the autumn of 1942, Barry decided to return to New York. As a gesture of goodwill, Chaplin paid for her train ticket; he also gave Barry $5,000 to settle her debts. Accompanied by her mother, Gertrude, Barry left Los Angeles in early October.

Later that month, Chaplin himself traveled to New York to deliver a speech on behalf of Russian War Relief. While he was there, he permitted Barry to visit him at his suite at the Waldorf-Astoria. On this occasion, he recalled, her manner was pleasant and easygoing, but Chaplin kept the reunion brief. The window-smashing incident had convinced him that Barry was mentally disturbed.

Shortly after his return to California, Chaplin was introduced to a seventeen-year-old aspiring actress named Oona O'Neill. Shy and very attractive, she was the daughter of American playwright Eugene O'Neill. Despite the thirty-five years that separated them in age, Chaplin and Oona fell in love almost immediately. According to Charles, Jr., "Whenever Oona was with our father a rapt expression would come into her eyes. . . . She worshipped him, drinking in every word he spoke, whether it was about his latest script, the weather or some bit of philosophy."[9]

In May 1943, to Chaplin's dismay, Joan Barry reappeared in Los Angeles. According to the actor, she came to his house to tell him that she was pregnant and needed money. Chaplin, refusing to give in to such blackmail, ordered her to leave the premises; when she refused, he called the police and had her arrested. Shortly thereafter, Barry told her story to gossip columnist Hedda Hopper, who shared it with her readers on June 3. That same day, Barry filed a paternity suit against Chaplin, claiming that he was the father of her unborn child.

At this point, Chaplin's lawyer discreetly suggested that Oona O'Neill leave town for a while. Chaplin's private life would be coming under scrutiny, and it might not look good for him to be associating with a seventeen-year-old. But Oona refused to go. She was determined to support Chaplin, no matter how upsetting the Barry scandal became. Later that month, on June 16, she and the actor were married in Carpinteria, a small town near Santa Barbara.

By making Oona his bride, Chaplin hoped to demonstrate to the public that his basic values were sound, that he was at heart a family man who believed in the sanctity of marriage. Unfortunately, the Chaplin-O'Neill wedding had the opposite effect. With the paternity suit still fresh in mind, many Americans decided that they were offended, even repulsed, by Chaplin's morality. The weeks that followed his wedding were a tense and anxious period for the comedian. "Occasionally," he said, "I would sink into a deep depression, feeling that I had . . . the hate of a whole nation upon me and that my film career was lost."

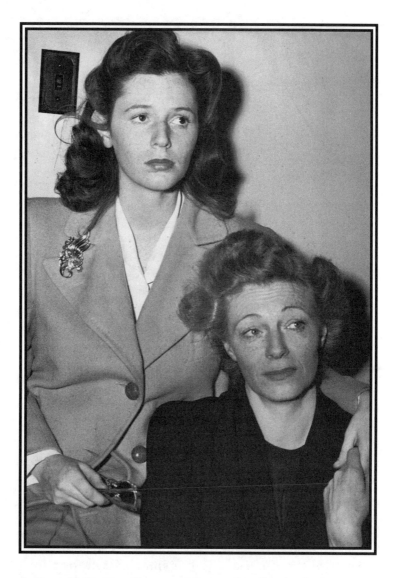

In June 1943, Joan Barry and her mother discuss the details of Joan's paternity suit against Chaplin. Although a blood test showed that Charlie was not the child's father, a jury decided against the 54-year-old star, and a court ordered him to pay child support.

On October 2, 1943, Joan Barry gave birth to a girl named Carol Ann. Blood samples taken four months later would prove that Chaplin could not have fathered the baby. Barry, however, refused to drop the paternity suit. After further legal complications for Chaplin, the case finally went to court in December 1944. Every newspaper in America covered the story. According to *Newsweek* magazine, it was the "biggest public relations scandal since the Fatty Arbuckle murder trial in 1921."

To represent her, Barry had hired a tough, seventy-seven-year-old lawyer named Joseph Scott. In the courtroom, Scott did his best to vilify Chaplin, referring to him as a "gray-headed old buzzard," a "reptile," and "a cheap Cockney cad." Scott's final words to the jury trembled with indignation: "There has been no one to stop Chaplin in his lecherous conduct all these years—except you. Wives and mothers all over the country are watching to see you stop him dead in his tracks. You'll sleep well the night you give this baby a name."[10]

After long deliberation, the jury announced that it could not reach a verdict. Barry and her lawyer insisted on a retrial, which opened in April 1945. This time, Scott's arguments carried the day: the jury decided against Chaplin, who was ordered by the court to pay $75 per week to Carol Ann until she reached the age of twenty-one. The case's outcome, said one Los Angeles attorney, was "a landmark in the miscarriage of justice."

In his book *Chaplin and American Culture*, Charles J. Maland discusses at length the damaging effect the Barry scandal had on Chaplin's reputation in America. According to Maland, "the Joan Barry case was to lie close to the surface of the American public imagination for a long time. . . . Chaplin's star image, which at one time seemed unassailable, was under attack."[11] Unfortunately for the comedian, the paternity trials would soon be followed by another, much more serious ordeal, one that in Maland's words "would eventually separate him from the country he had called home since 1913."

10

THE PATH
TO EXILE

IN 1946, AFTER TWO YEARS' work, Charlie Chaplin finished writing the script for his next motion picture, *Monsieur Verdoux*. Despite the humiliations he had suffered during the Joan Barry trials, he refused to believe that his career was in jeopardy or that his fans had abandoned him. One "good comedy," he maintained, "would solve all my troubles." Unfortunately, *Monsieur Verdoux* would solve nothing. Upon its release in 1947, it would prove to be a box-office disaster, a film that served only to antagonize and confuse a large segment of the American public. As one reviewer wrote, "I am bewildered by it and disappointed."

Subtitled "a comedy of murder," *Monsieur Verdoux* opens with a close-up of a tombstone bearing the inscription "Henri Verdoux 1880–1937." In a voice-over, Chaplin (as Verdoux) explains that for years he was a bank teller in Paris. Then, through no fault of his own, he lost his job during the depression. In order to support his crippled wife and child, Verdoux was "forced" to adopt a new profession for himself—that of marrying wealthy women and then murdering them for their money.

117

As played by Chaplin, Verdoux is a fascinating and complex character, a man who has murdered thirteen women but is careful not to step on a worm while trimming the rose bushes in his garden. Personally, he dislikes his "job," but he doesn't consider it sinful or wrong. The world is a ruthless place, he says, and in order to survive, one's behavior must be equally ruthless.

Much of the comedy in the film concerns Verdoux's relationship with Annabella Bonheur (Martha Raye). A seemingly indestructible woman, Annabella unwittingly foils Verdoux's every attempt to murder her. When Verdoux takes her out in a rowboat, for instance, intending to drown her, it is he himself who ends up falling overboard.

Verdoux's schemes ultimately catch up with him. Toward the end of the film, he is arrested and brought to trial. In the courtroom, Verdoux expresses no remorse for what he has done, nor does he believe that he should be punished. As he explains to the judge, his behavior is only a reflection of modern society, where profit is valued more highly than human life. In any case, he says, his crimes are insignificant compared to those the government commits—especially in wartime, when millions of innocent people are slaughtered in the name of patriotism. "As a mass killer, I am an amateur by comparison. . . . To be shocked by the nature of my crime is nothing but a pretence . . . a sham!"[1]

Later, in his cell, Verdoux cynically defends his violent profession: "Wars, conflict—it's all business. One murder makes a villain; millions, a hero. Numbers sanctify!" On that chilly, philosophical note, Verdoux is led away to his execution.

While Chaplin was producing *Monsieur Verdoux*, he and Mary Pickford learned that United Artists was $1 million in debt. Pickford was extremely concerned about the deficit, but Chaplin told her not to worry. He was confident that *Monsieur Verdoux* would be a box-office smash. One official at United Artists had assured him that it would gross at least $12 million.

The world premiere of *Monsieur Verdoux* was held in New York City on April 11, 1947. According to Chaplin, "There was an uneasy atmosphere in the theatre that night, a feeling that the audience had come to prove something." During the screening, some people laughed, but others hissed, and Chaplin became so upset that he left after the first reel. At a supper party later that night, very few people complimented him on his new film.

Monsieur Verdoux is now considered one of Chaplin's cleverest and most sophisticated comedies. According to critic Leonard Maltin, the film "was years ahead of its time; its wry humor and pacifist sentiments make it quite contemporary when seen today." But in 1947, when *Monsieur Verdoux* was first released, it was a critical disappointment and a financial failure. American audiences were not amused by the subject matter, nor did they care for the bitter tone of the script. Verdoux's courtroom speech, in particular, made many people uncomfortable. Was Chaplin suggesting that murder was morally acceptable? Or was he criticizing the government—and if so, which government?

This question, unfortunately, would persuade people to take a closer look at Chaplin's politics, especially his views concerning Communist Russia. To understand Chaplin's political troubles, it is important to remember that, in 1947, the United States and Russia were no longer allies; the Russians, in fact, had replaced the Nazis as America's most hated adversary. In the words of one historian, Americans in the late 1940s were feeling "anxious to the point of paranoia about the threat of Communism." This shift in the political climate did not bode well for Chaplin, who had been making sympathetic remarks about Russia ever since the 1920s.

A few days after the New York premiere, Chaplin held a large press conference at the Gotham Hotel to promote *Monsieur Verdoux.* Hundreds of journalists showed up, but to Chaplin's dismay only a handful bothered to ask about the film. The majority had come to explore his political beliefs.

"Are you a Communist?" one reporter asked.

"Life is becoming so technical," Chaplin answered, "that if you step off the curb with your left foot, they accuse you of being a Communist. . . . I've never belonged to any political party in my life, and I have never voted in my life!"[2]

The reporters were not satisfied. What about the speeches he had made in 1942 on Russia's behalf? Was he a Communist sympathizer? "I don't know what you mean," Chaplin said. "During the war, I sympathized very much with Russia. . . . I think that she helped contribute a considerable amount of fighting and dying to bring victory to the Allies. In that sense I am sympathetic."[3]

He was then asked about his friendship with composer Hanns Eisler. Did he know that Eisler was a Communist? Chaplin's answer was testy: "Nobody is going to tell me whom to like or dislike. We haven't come to that yet."

"Why haven't you become a citizen?" a reporter demanded.

"I see no reason to change my nationality," Chaplin replied. "I consider myself a citizen of the world." (This comment, he recalled, created "quite a stir.")

The questions kept coming. Was he a patriot, and if so, how would he define his patriotism? Why had he not contributed more vigorously to the war effort? Chaplin put up with the grilling for as long as he could; then, abruptly, he brought the meeting to an end. "I'm sorry, ladies and gentlemen. I thought this . . . was to be an interview about my film; instead it has turned into a political brawl, so I have nothing further to say."[4]

"What a moral nonentity this Chaplin is!" thundered the *Los Angeles Herald-Express*. "He has been what he terms 'a paying guest' in this country too long. He has shirked every responsibility of the American citizen. He brags that he has never cast a vote in his life. Even permitting him to remain in the United States insults the intelligence of the American people."[5]

Two months later, in June, Chaplin was denounced in Congress by Representative John E. Rankin of Mississippi, who was outraged by the actor's "refusal" to become an American citizen. Chaplin and his "*loathsome*" pictures, Rankin said, "[are] detrimental to the moral fabric of America. . . . He should be deported and gotten rid of at once."

To add to his troubles, Chaplin learned that he would soon be called to Washington to appear before the House Un-American Activities Committee (HUAC). At the hearing, he would be questioned about his alleged "communistic leanings." In late July, the actor fired off a snide telegram to Washington: "While you are preparing your engraved subpoena I will give you a hint on where I stand. I am not a Communist. I am a peacemonger."[6]

A few months later, to Chaplin's surprise, HUAC informed him that he need not come to Washington—his testimony would not be required after all. The comedian was disappointed. Had he been called to appear, he said, "I'd have turned up in my tramp outfit . . . and when I was questioned I'd have used all sorts of comic business to make a laughing stock of the inquisitors. . . . If I had [testified], the whole Un-American Activities thing would have been laughed out of existence."[7]

But conservative Americans were in no mood to laugh along with Charlie Chaplin. In Memphis, Tennessee, *Monsieur Verdoux* was banned from the screen; in other cities, pressure groups threatened to boycott any theater that dared to show it. As a result, box-office receipts plummeted. By the end of the year, *Monsieur Verdoux* had grossed only $162,000.

The year 1947 ended badly for Chaplin when syndicated columnist Westbrook Pegler accused him of being a Communist sympathizer, a tax cheat, and "a slacker in both World Wars." Though Pegler could not substantiate his accusations, many Americans were quick to believe him. According to one biographer, attacks such as Pegler's continued "to chip away at [Chaplin's] declining star image. The reputation that once had seemed a pillar of marble now seemed composed of sandstone."[8]

Throughout this period, Chaplin's one consolation was his family. Oona had given birth to their first child, Geraldine, in the summer of 1944. The next few years would see the arrival of three more children: Michael (born in 1946), Josephine (1949), and Victoria (1951). Chaplin also enjoyed a warm relationship with his elder sons, Charles, Jr., and Sydney, both of whom had served in Europe during World War II.

In early 1948, Chaplin began to write the story for his next motion picture, *Limelight*. "For I was optimistic," he said, "and still not convinced that . . . the American people . . . could be so politically conscious or so humorless as to boycott anyone that could amuse them."[9] The comedian spent more than three years preparing the script for *Limelight*, which went into production in November 1951.

In *Limelight*, Chaplin played an aging music hall comedian named Calvero. Once he was the toast of London; now, an alcoholic, he fears that he has lost his touch and can no longer make people laugh. At the start of the film, a drunken Calvero smells gas in the hallway of his seedy boardinghouse. Breaking down a door, he manages to save a young woman named Terry Ambrose (Claire Bloom), who has tried to commit suicide in the flat below his. Out of compassion, Calvero takes her back to his own apartment and calls a doctor.

Terry, it turns out, is not grateful for the older man's help. An aspiring ballerina, she has developed a mysterious paralysis that has left her unable to walk. Over the next several months, Calvero nurses her back to health, all the while giving her reasons to go on living. In the process, Calvero discovers his own sense of self-worth.

In time, Terry regains the use of her legs and, with renewed confidence, continues her dancing career. Her success inspires Calvero to attempt his own comeback,

In Limelight *(1952), Charlie portrays an aging music hall comedian who befriends a ballerina (Claire Bloom). In the United States, the American Legion organized a nationwide boycott of the film because of Chaplin's alleged Communist affiliations and a perceived lack of morals.*

but, sadly, his career continues to fade. Terry, meanwhile, befriends a handsome young composer named Neville (Sydney Chaplin, Charlie's son). When Calvero observes that Terry is falling in love with Neville, he disappears from her life for six months. Unable to secure any theatrical engagements, he becomes a "busker," a street entertainer.

Near the end of the film, the owner of the Empire Theatre decides to stage a benefit for Calvero, at which the comedian will perform. It is Calvero's last chance to win back his old-time fans. Before a packed house, he performs a delightful routine with another aging vaudevillian (Buster Keaton). This sequence—the only time Chaplin and Keaton ever performed together—is one of the few genuinely funny moments in *Limelight*. Keaton, playing a nearsighted pianist, does his best to accompany Calvero on the violin, but his sheet music keeps falling to the ground and the piano is hilariously out of tune. Calvero, meanwhile, discovers that his right leg has mysteriously begun to shorten. Bewildered, he manages to shake it out to its regular length, only to have the left leg do the same. Then, to his shock, *both* legs begin to shrink.

After much foolery, the act climaxes when Calvero crashes into a large bass drum, from which he takes his bows. At that moment, unbeknownst to the audience, he suffers a heart attack. Laid out on a cot, Calvero dies in the wings while his beautiful protégée, Terry, is performing onstage.

During the making of *Limelight*, Chaplin told his family that it would be his last and his greatest film. At sixty-two, he still enjoyed his work, but as an artist he no longer felt welcome in Hollywood. In *My Father, Charlie Chaplin*, Charles, Jr., remembered this period with a certain sadness. By 1952, he said, his father had become a political outcast: "It was no longer considered a privilege to be a guest at the home of Charlie Chaplin. Many people were actually afraid to be seen there lest they, too, should become suspect. . . . I think my father must have been the loneliest man in Hollywood those days.

"It was in that spirit, a spirit of haunting farewell, that he [worked] on *Limelight*, the nostalgic story of a pantomimist who had once been widely acclaimed but had fallen in later years into disfavor and eclipse."[10]

Chaplin had originally planned to shoot part of *Limelight* in London. He changed his mind, however, when he learned that, because of his alleged Communism, he might not be permitted to return to America. Actress Claire Bloom wrote that she, too, was aware of Chaplin's sensitive position: "In the last few years he had been deeply homesick, he said, but he didn't dare to leave. . . . His family, home, studios, money—everything was in America."[11]

It was an unpleasant situation, one that Chaplin could not tolerate for long. Upon finishing *Limelight* in early 1952, he announced that in September he and his family would travel to London for the world premiere. Before Chaplin could leave the country, he had to apply for a reentry permit from the Immigration and Naturalization Service (INS); the permit was issued in mid-July. Two months later, on September 18, the Chaplin family set sail for England aboard the *Queen Elizabeth*.

The following day, while the ship was at sea, Chaplin received disturbing news. In Washington, Attorney General James McGranery had ordered the INS to revoke Chaplin's reentry permit. Before the comedian could return to America, he would have to meet with INS officials and answer questions about his moral and political conduct. In a press statement, McGranery called Chaplin "an unsavory character" who in the past had exhibited "a leering, sneering attitude" toward his host country.

Chaplin was shocked by this turn of events. He was tempted, he said, to denounce the American government, but after thinking it over, he decided to keep silent: "Everything I possessed was in the States and I was terrified they might find a way of confiscating it." Upon his arrival in Southampton, England, Chaplin told the press that he hoped to return to America: "I am very philosophical about it all. . . . I do not want to create any revolution. . . . I'm an individualist, and I believe in liberty. That is as far as my political convictions go."[12]

In America, a number of people, including Mary Pickford and Buster Keaton, came to Chaplin's defense. Many prominent journalists, however, applauded the attorney general's decision. In Hollywood, Hedda Hopper reported that most people were "dancing in the street for joy" at the news. Chaplin, she went on to say, might be a good actor, "but that doesn't give him the right to go against our customs, to abhor everything we stand for, to throw our hospitality back in our faces. . . . Good riddance to bad company."[13] Gossip columnist Louella Parsons was one of the few to express any sympathy: "How very, very sad that the fantastic success story of Charles Spencer Chaplin is destined to end on such a tragic note."

11
SWISS EXILE

ON THE EVENING OF OCTOBER 16, 1952, *Limelight* received its world premiere at the Odeon Theatre in London. Princess Margaret was in attendance, but according to *Variety*, it was Charlie Chaplin who was accorded the most applause. Two weeks later, the comedian and his wife traveled to Paris, where the French government elevated Chaplin to the rank of Officer of the Legion of Honor. He was also decorated by the Italian government on a subsequent visit to Rome. Chaplin said that everywhere he and Oona went, they were treated "like conquering heroes."

In Washington, meanwhile, the attorney general's office announced that it had "a pretty good case" against Chaplin, but this was untrue. The government, in fact, had no case at all. Despite a lengthy investigation, the FBI had uncovered no evidence to suggest that Chaplin posed a threat to national security. Had he returned to fight the charges, he would almost certainly have been readmitted to the country.

One week after its London premiere, *Limelight* opened in two theaters in New York City. While the reviews were favorable, most critics felt that the film should have been funnier. The screenplay was also criticized for being too wordy. "From the first reel of *Limelight*," wrote Walter Kerr, "it is perfectly clear that Chaplin now wants to talk, that he *loves* to talk, that in this film he intends to do little *but* talk."[1]

Unfortunately, few people in America had the opportunity to see *Limelight*. In early 1953, the film was subjected to a nationwide boycott by the American Legion. As a result, only a handful of exhibitors were willing to book it. In most European countries, however, *Limelight* proved to be a box-office hit. Eventually earning more than $5 million worldwide, it was financially the most successful of all of Chaplin's films.

By late 1952, the actor and his wife had decided not to return to the United States, after all. They would settle in Switzerland, they said, and raise the children there. In mid-November, Oona flew to Los Angeles to retrieve her husband's savings and to wrap up their business affairs. Upon her return to Europe, she and Chaplin purchased a large, fifteen-room villa in the Swiss town of Corsier, near Vevey. The Manoir de Ban was a beautiful, three-story home, situated on thirty-seven acres of land. At first, Chaplin worried that he and Oona could not afford to maintain such a large estate. They soon discovered, however, that the household expenses were well within their budget.

To Chaplin's delight, the family continued to grow. In August 1953, Oona gave birth to a son named Eugene. Three more children were to follow: Jane (born in 1957), Annette (1959), and Christopher (1962). Shortly after Chaplin's banishment, Oona was asked by the press to describe her husband. What was it like being married to Charlie Chaplin? "Charlie is a half-and-half personality," she ventured. "One half is difficult—the other easy. But I find we manage very happily. He is an attentive husband and a wonderful father."[2]

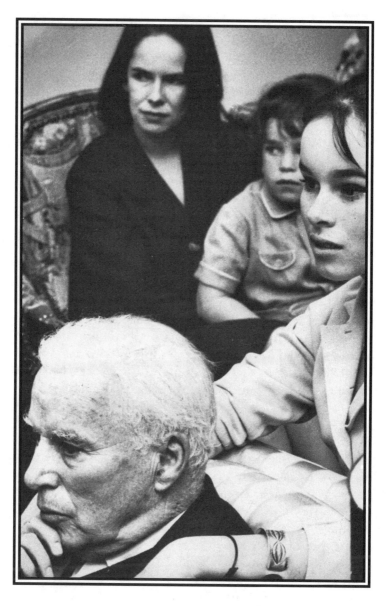

Charlie relaxes at a 1959 family gathering. Chaplin married Oona O'Neill in 1943, and the couple settled down on an estate in Corsier, Switzerland, where they reared their eight children.

In April 1953, Chaplin paid a visit to the American embassy in Geneva, where he formally surrendered his reentry permit. He told the press that it saddened him to take this action, but he did not wish to live in a country "in which liberal-minded individuals can be singled out and persecuted." Shortly thereafter, Oona gave up her American citizenship and became a British subject. Chaplin's final ties to America were severed in 1955 when he sold his United Artists stock for $1.1 million.

Though Chaplin was no longer living in the United States, his behavior continued to irritate the American people. As one of Switzerland's most distinguished residents, he was often sought out by celebrities and well-known rulers of state. In 1954, for instance, he was entertained in Geneva by Chou En-Lai, the prime minister of Communist China. Two years later, at a Soviet reception in London, he enjoyed a warm conversation with Russian leader Nikita Khrushchev. Incidents such as these prompted one American magazine to accuse Chaplin of "doing all he can to make the world weep bitterly and worry its head off. After living in the United States forty years, Chaplin has openly joined our enemy, the Soviet slave masters."[3]

In his autobiography, Chaplin discussed how he had come to lose the affection of the American public. He realized that he had annoyed many people by never applying for U.S. citizenship. He had also antagonized the government by expressing his contempt for the House Un-American Activities Committee. But his greatest source of trouble, he maintained, was in "being a nonconformist. Although I am not a Communist I refused to fall in line by hating them."

Despite the comfortable life he enjoyed with his family in Corsier, retirement did not agree with Chaplin. Therefore, in 1954 he began to write the script for his eightieth motion picture, *A King in New York*. The film was shot in London in 1956 and released in Europe the following year.

In the film, Chaplin played the title character, King

Shahdov of Estrovia. When a revolution forces him from his throne, Shahdov seeks refuge in America, where he hopes to share his plans for world peace with the government. During his brief stay in New York, the king is exposed to various aspects of American life, including wide-screen movies, TV commercials, plastic surgery, and rock-and-roll music. In one amusing scene, Shahdov and his U.S. ambassador (Oliver Johnston) visit a noisy restaurant. They are seated next to the orchestra. The king tries to order caviar and turtle soup, but the waiter is unable to hear him over the music. To make himself understood, Shahdov resorts to pantomime, impersonating first a sturgeon, then a slow-moving turtle. The sight of Chaplin transforming himself into a sturgeon is unforgettable, a vivid example of his unparalleled gift for pantomimic comedy.

As the story develops, King Shahdov is exposed to yet another discouraging aspect of American life: the government's paranoic fear of Communism. During a visit to a progressive school, he meets a young boy named Rupert Macabee (Michael Chaplin, Charlie's son), whose parents are being investigated by HUAC. A radical, Rupert refuses to cooperate with the FBI by answering questions about his parents' political beliefs. As a result of his friendship with Rupert, the king himself is subpoenaed to appear before HUAC. On his way to the hearing, Shahdov gets his finger stuck in a fire hose. A guard unwittingly turns on the water and Shahdov, unable to control the hose, drenches his grim-faced inquisitors. Fed up with the American way of life, the king eventually decides to return to Estrovia, where peace has been restored.

Because of its anti-American sentiments, *A King in New York* was not released in the United States. It was, however, reviewed in a number of American newspapers and magazines. Nearly every critic panned the film. "*A King in New York* . . . is dismaying from any position you choose to take," said the *New Republic*. "If you look for comedy, it is almost entirely missing: and when it turns up it is usually inept. If you look for pathos, you look in vain: Chaplin tries for the pathetic a dozen times, but he never comes close."[4]

Shortly after finishing *A King in New York*, Chaplin began to write his autobiography. In 1960, he told an acquaintance that he had nearly finished the book, but another four years would pass before it was ready for publication. While Chaplin was writing his memoirs, the political climate in the United States began to shift once again. America's relations with the Soviet Union were gradually improving, and much of the postwar hysteria over Communism had evaporated.

The American social climate was changing, as well. According to one historian, "an increasing number of [citizens] were questioning . . . many of the assumptions and practices of the previous fifteen years." These changes, both political and social, would do much to rehabilitate Chaplin's image. As early as 1960, there was a tendency in the American press to present the actor in a more favorable light.

While Chaplin was writing his autobiography, comedian Buster Keaton was working on his. After years of neglect by the industry, Keaton was starting to enjoy a comeback. Film buffs were calling him a genius, and some of his silent features (including *The General*) were being hailed as masterpieces. In April 1960, Buster Keaton received a special Academy Award for his film work. That same year, his autobiography appeared in bookstores.

In *My Wonderful World of Slapstick*, Keaton had good things to say about Chaplin's work as a comedian. Nevertheless, he felt that in the early 1920s, Chaplin started to take himself too seriously: "It was his misfortune to believe what the critics wrote about him. They said he was a genius . . . and from that time on . . . [he] tried to behave, think, and talk like an intellectual."[5]

Keaton also took the actor to task for his political beliefs. "Charlie is a stubborn man," he wrote, "and when his right to talk favorably about communism was challenged he simply got bullheaded about it. . . . [There are] rumors that Charlie would like to get back to America. I hope he makes it. Even more I hope he keeps his promise to start making pictures again."[6]

In the summer of 1962, Chaplin was awarded an honorary degree by Oxford University. The ceremony, which attracted a huge crowd, made the front page of the *New York Times*. A few days later, the *Times* encouraged President Kennedy to lift the long-standing ban on Chaplin: "We do not believe the Republic would be in danger . . . if yesterday's unforgotten little tramp were allowed to amble down the gangplank of an American port."[7]

The White House did not respond to this suggestion. Nevertheless, Chaplin had reason to believe that if he made a peaceful overture to the American people, it might be accepted. In November 1963, he allowed the Plaza Theater in New York to hold a Chaplin film series, in which nearly all of his feature-length comedies were rereleased over an eleven-month period.

New Yorkers flocked to see such classics as *The Gold Rush* and *City Lights*, but the biggest hit of the festival was *Monsieur Verdoux*. Released in July 1964, it set a weekend box-office record at the Plaza. The film, said one critic, "[is a] classic that we are at last privileged to appreciate after its abortive debut 17 years ago." This time around, audiences were not put off by the grisly subject matter. Nor were they offended by Verdoux's cynical view of capitalist society. In America there was a growing tendency to criticize the government, and Verdoux's impassioned courtroom speech struck a responsive chord among many viewers.

The latter-day success of *Verdoux* was not overlooked by the American press. To *Newsweek* magazine, it was a clear sign that Chaplin's star was rising: "What has changed—at least in New York, and probably throughout the country—is the atmosphere. Chaplin is no longer a villain. A new generation has grown up, receptive to his artistry and eager for his gift of laughter. This very change affects the way we now view the film."[8]

In September 1964, while the series was still playing, Chaplin's autobiography was published by Simon and

Schuster. More than five hundred pages in length, it was judged by *Time* magazine to be "one of the richest publishing coups of the century." The reviewers were unanimous in both their praise and their criticism. Everyone enjoyed the first eleven chapters, in which Chaplin depicts his unhappy youth, his touring days with the Karno Company, and the twelve months he spent with Mack Sennett at Keystone.

The rest of the book, however, is less compelling. As biographer David Robinson observes, "From the twelfth chapter onwards . . . Chaplin is much more concerned to describe his social life . . . than to reveal anything" about his film career. Nor was the actor forthcoming about his torturous, two-year marriage to Lita Grey (Lita's name, in fact, appears nowhere in the text). Chaplin was also criticized for his pompous writing style.

Despite these drawbacks, *My Autobiography* was an extremely popular book, leaping to the number-one spot on the *New York Times* best-seller list. In addition to reviewing the work, some critics brought up the subject of Chaplin's exile. One journalist spoke of the government's "cowardly revocation of his re-entry permit." Another believed that "the persecution of Chaplin in the name of American patriotism . . . is a scandal this era is saddled with forever." Comments such as these helped pave the way for Chaplin's eventual return to the United States.

Encouraged by the success of his autobiography, Chaplin began to prepare his next motion picture, *A Countess from Hong Kong.* A romantic comedy, *Countess* was a reworking of *Stowaway*, the script Chaplin had written for Paulette Goddard in 1936. To play the leads, Chaplin cast two of Hollywood's biggest stars, Marlon Brando and Sophia Loren. To fill supporting roles, he hired Tippi Hedren and Margaret Rutherford, as well as his thirty-nine-year-old son, Sydney, who had just played opposite Barbra Streisand in the Broadway production of *Funny Girl.* Shooting began in England in early 1966.

In the film, Brando plays a wealthy American ambassador named Ogden Mears. On a visit to China, he meets a beautiful countess, Natascha Alexandroff (Loren). A Russian émigré, the countess now works as a dancer at a Hong Kong nightspot. When Mears sails back to America, Natascha stows away in his stateroom. Naturally, Mears discovers her; the rest of the film consists of tiresome sight gags as the ambassador tries to keep Natascha's presence a secret.

Because of the high-voltage casting of Loren and Brando, *A Countess from Hong Kong* received a great deal of advance publicity. Loren thoroughly enjoyed working with Chaplin, whom she idolized, but Brando was miserable. In his 1994 autobiography, the actor called Chaplin "an egotistical tyrant and a penny-pincher. He harassed people when they were late, and scolded them unmercifully to work faster." By the time shooting was completed, the two men were barely on speaking terms.

A Countess from Hong Kong was released in 1967 to dreadful reviews. "I wish I could say some nice things about [it]," said one critic, "but *A Countess* . . . is so old-fashioned and dull that one can hardly believe it was made now." *Time* magazine agreed, dismissing the movie as "the worst ever made by Charlie Chaplin."

In April 1969, the comedian celebrated his eightieth birthday. His health was beginning to fail, but he assured reporters that he had no intention of retiring. In the early 1970s, Chaplin rereleased most of his silent films, including *The Kid* and *The Circus,* neither of which had been screened since the 1920s. For both films, he composed a new musical score.

In 1971, Chaplin was honored at the prestigious Cannes Film Festival in France. At the same time, the French government made him a Commander of the Legion of Honor. The following year, he was invited to return to Los Angeles to accept a special Academy Award. Though Chaplin feared his presence might stir up controversy, he agreed to make the trip.

He and Oona arrived in New York City on April 3, 1972. They were met at the airport by more than one hundred reporters and photographers. As Chaplin disembarked from the jet, he smiled and waved to the crowd; then, lifting his fingers to his lips, he blew a heartfelt kiss—once, twice, three times. "The return of the great mime," said the *New York Times,* "was a scene worthy of the silent films."

During Chaplin's brief stay in New York, Mayor John Lindsay presented him with the Handel Medallion, the city's highest cultural award. The Chaplins also attended a lavish party given by Gloria Vanderbilt Cooper, where they chatted with such celebrities as author Truman Capote and silent film star Lillian Gish. But the highlight of the New York stay was the April 4 black-tie "Salute to Charlie Chaplin" at Lincoln Center. After *The Idle Class* and *The Kid* had been screened, more than 2,700 people gave Chaplin a lengthy standing ovation. "This is my renaissance," the actor said, with tears in his eyes. "I'm being born again."

A few days later, he and Oona flew to Los Angeles to attend the Academy Awards ceremony at the Dorothy Chandler Pavilion. On the night of April 10, millions of viewers watched as Chaplin accepted a special Oscar for his "incalculable effect in making motion pictures the art form of the century." The eighty-two-year-old was visibly moved as he stood at the podium, clutching his statuette. "Words seem so futile, so feeble," he said. "This is a very emotional moment for me. I can only thank you, thank you for inviting me here. You are wonderful . . . sweet people."[9]

Actor Jack Lemmon then handed Chaplin a derby hat and cane. For most viewers, it was an unforgettable moment. After more than twenty years of bitterness and acrimony, Chaplin had made his peace with the American public. According to the *New York Times,* "The glittering audience rose and cheered for several minutes," and the evening concluded with everyone singing "Smile," the theme song from *Modern Times.*

The last few years of the comedian's life were quiet, but not idle. In 1974, he wrote another book, *My Life in Pictures,* a lavishly illustrated companion volume to *My Autobiography.* The following year, in March, he was knighted by Queen Elizabeth II. By then, Chaplin's health had

On April 10, 1972, Charlie poses for photographs after receiving a special Oscar for his "incalculable effect in making motion pictures the art form of the century."

become frail; suffering from gout, he was unable to walk without aid. Nevertheless, he insisted that retirement was out of the question. "I can't stop," he said. "Ideas just keep popping into my head."

In 1976, the year before he died, Chaplin decided to resurrect *A Woman of Paris*, his 1923 drama starring Edna Purviance and Adolphe Menjou. For the rerelease, he trimmed a few scenes and composed a musical score. The film was shown at the Museum of Modern Art in New York in January 1977. Said *Newsweek*: "[It is] an elegantly glittering tale . . . of passion, money and art—the trinity that ruled Chaplin's sensibility."[10]

That same year, the American Film Institute asked its members to select the fifty finest American-made films. When the results were tabulated, only five silents were chosen: D. W. Griffith's *The Birth of a Nation* and *Intolerance*; Buster Keaton's Civil War comedy, *The General*; and Chaplin's *The Gold Rush* and *City Lights*.

It was on this note of quiet satisfaction that Chaplin's life drew to a close. After a career that had spanned more than seventy-five years, the comedian died at his home in Corsier on December 25, 1977. The funeral was held two days later. It was a small gathering: Chaplin had specifically asked that no crowds be present.

Meanwhile, tributes poured in from around the world. Stage and film actor Laurence Olivier considered Chaplin "perhaps the greatest actor of all time." French director René Clair called him "a monument of the cinema. . . . He inspired practically every film maker." Comedian Bob Hope's comment was simple, but fitting: "We were fortunate to have lived in his time."

In his 1973 book *The Great Movies*, William Bayer wrote that "no comic is as loved as Chaplin. . . . He did so many things so well, developed and changed so many times . . . that the richness of his work may be mined by every taste."[11] During his long and distinguished career, Charlie Chaplin appeared in eighty-one films, at least twenty of which are considered classics. *The Kid, The Gold Rush, City Lights,* and *Modern Times* have lost none of their appeal. For directing these gems—and for creating the character of the Little Tramp—Chaplin has rightly been called "one of the half-dozen immortals of the American screen."

In recent years, many people have come to prefer the silent films of Buster Keaton to those of Charlie Chaplin. Film historians Kevin Brownlow and John Kobal are quick to point out that "Chaplin was very much a man of his time. Keaton, unsentimental and cynical, is more a man of ours. During his career, Chaplin received an extraordinary degree of praise, and audiences therefore expect more from his films than anyone else's."

While defending Keaton's work, Brownlow and Kobal firmly believe that Chaplin was the superior artist: "Fashion will change again, and so long as Chaplin's films survive, so will his genius. He was, and he will always remain, the greatest comedian in the history of the motion picture."[12]

*The Little Tramp and the gamine head for a brighter future
in the closing scene from* Modern Times.

SOURCE NOTES

CHAPTER ONE

1. Mack Sennett, as told to Cameron Shipp, *King of Comedy* (Garden City, New York: Doubleday, 1954; San Francisco: Mercury House, 1990), p. 148.
2. Ibid., p. 88.
3. Rose Wilder Lane, *Charlie Chaplin's Own Story* (Indianapolis: Bobbs-Merrill, 1916), quoted in Donald W. McCaffrey, ed., *Focus on Chaplin* (Englewood Cliffs, NJ: Prentice-Hall, 1971), p. 31.
4. Charles Chaplin, *My Autobiography* (New York: Simon and Schuster, 1964; New York: Pocket Books, 1966), p. 146.
5. Sennett, p. 158. In 1995, at a British auction of film memorabilia, Chaplin's hat and cane were sold for $68,720.
6. Chaplin, p. 148.
7. Chaplin did appear in the film, but not dressed as the Tramp.
8. Sennett, p. 156.
9. John Montgomery, *Comedy Films* (London: Allen &

Unwin, 1954), quoted in McCaffrey, pp. 16–17.
10. Sennett, p. 190.

CHAPTER TWO

1. John McCabe, *Charlie Chaplin* (Garden City, N.Y.: Doubleday, 1978), p. 1.
2. *American Magazine* (November 1918), quoted in David Robinson, *Chaplin: His Life and Art* (New York: McGraw-Hill, 1985), p. 18.
3. *Pearson's Weekly* (September 21, 1921), quoted in Robinson, p. 22.
4. Chaplin, p. 31.
5. Ibid., p. 33.
6. James Card, *Seductive Cinema: The Art of Silent Film* (New York: Knopf, 1994), pp. 15–16.
7. Richard Griffith and Arthur Mayer, *The Movies* (New York: Bonanza Books, 1957), p. 3.
8. Chaplin, p. 38.
9. McCabe, p. 17.
10. Robinson, p. 40.
11. Ibid., p. 42.
12. Chaplin, pp. 73–74.

CHAPTER THREE

1 Robinson, p. 47.
2. *Glasgow Weekly Herald* (September 10, 1921), quoted in Robinson, p. 66.
3. Chaplin, p. 97.
4. Robinson, pp. 77–78.
5. Ibid., pg. 81, and McCabe, p. 35.
6. McCabe, p. 39.
7. Ibid., p. 40, and Robinson, p. 89.
8. McCabe, p. 41, and Robinson, pp. 92–93.
9. McCabe, p. 46, and Robinson, p. 102, and Chaplin, p. 141. The wording of the telegram varies from source to source.
10. Chaplin, p. 142.

CHAPTER FOUR

1. Sennett, p. 152.
2. Chaplin, p. 146.
3. Sennett, p. 153.
4. Ibid., pp. 157–58.
5. Chaplin, p. 151.
6. Ibid., p. 162. Chaplin exaggerates here. There were a number of writers employed at Keystone, whose job it was to come up with stories. There was also a separate "gag room," where jokes and comedy routines were developed.
7. Robinson, pp. 131–33.
8. Gloria Swanson, *Swanson on Swanson* (New York: Random House, 1980), pp. 40–41.
9. McCabe, p. 76.
10. Robinson, p. 146.
11. Terry Ramsaye, *Reel Life* (March 4, 1916), quoted in Robinson, p. 157. Ramsaye calculated that Chaplin's salary came to $77.55 per hour "and if he should need a nickel for a carfare it only takes two seconds to earn it."
12. Chaplin, p. 189.

CHAPTER FIVE

1. *Harper's Weekly* (May 6, 1916), quoted in McCaffrey, pp. 69–70.
2. Theodore Huff, *Charlie Chaplin* (New York: Henry Schuman, 1951; New York: Pyramid Books, 1964), p. 63.
3. Robinson, p. 197.
4. Chaplin, p. 199.
5. McCabe, p. 95.
6. Robinson, p. 221.
7. McCabe, p. 103.
8. Chaplin, pp. 248, 257.
9. Robinson, p. 252.
10. Huff, p. 79. The divorce was granted in November 1920.

CHAPTER SIX

1. Huff, p. 107.
2. Chaplin, p. 259.
3. Rudi Blesh, *Keaton* (New York: Macmillan, 1966), p. 143.
4. *Exceptional Photoplays*, quoted in Charles J. Maland, *Chaplin and American Culture: The Evolution of a Star Image* (Princeton, N.J.: Princeton University Press, 1989), p. 59.
5. Robinson, p. 255.
6. Ibid., p. 280.
7. Ibid., p. 282. In 1922, Harper & Brothers published *My Trip Abroad*, Chaplin's book-length account of his European journey.
8. Pola Negri, *Memoirs of a Star* (Garden City, N.Y.: Doubleday, 1970), p. 180.
9. Chaplin, pp. 306, 318.
10. Robinson, p. 312.
11. Chaplin, p. 324.
12 Robinson, p. 329.

CHAPTER SEVEN

1. Chaplin, p. 327.
2. Ibid., p. 327.
3. Huff, p. 154.
4. Lita Grey Chaplin with Morton Cooper, *My Life with Chaplin* (New York: Bernard Geis Associates, 1966), p. 102.
5. Ibid., p. 98.
6. Ibid., p. 194.
7. In addition to the special statuette that Chaplin was given, *The Circus* received two Academy Award nominations: Best Actor and Best Comedy Direction. Chaplin won in neither category.
8. Lita Grey Chaplin, p. 226.
9. McCabe, p. 165.

CHAPTER EIGHT

1. Maland, p. 113.
2. Tom Dardis, *Harold Lloyd: The Man on the Clock* (New York: Viking Press, 1983), pp. 201–2.
3. James Agee, "Comedy's Greatest Era," *Life*, September 5, 1949, quoted in Robinson, p. 410. Agee's essay was responsible for launching a widespread revival of interest in the silent films of Chaplin, Keaton, Lloyd, and Harry Langdon.
4. Huff, p. 184.
5. Chaplin, p. 397.
6. The five-part series, "A Comedian Sees the World," appeared in *Woman's Home Companion* (September 1933 to January 1934). In 1933, the series was published in book form under the same title.
7. Chaplin, p. 415.
8. Charles Chaplin, Jr., with N. and M. Rau, *My Father, Charlie Chaplin* (New York: Random House, 1960; New York: Popular Library, 1961), pp. 88–89.
9. Roger Manvell, *Chaplin* (Boston: Little, Brown, 1974), p. 142.
10. Maland, p. 155.

CHAPTER NINE

1. *New York Times*, September 19, 1937, p. 5. According to this article, three factors were responsible for the Tramp's passing: the microphone, the popularity of Walt Disney's animated cartoons, and "that inevitable machine of destruction," progress.
2. Charles Chaplin, p. 426.
3. Ibid., pp. 433–34.
4. Maland, p. 181.
5. McCabe, p. 201.
6. Charles Chaplin, Jr., p. 192. Quoted in Maland, p. 197.
7. Charles Chaplin, pp. 443–44.
8. Maland, p. 191.

9. Charles Chaplin, Jr., p. 212.
10. Robinson, p. 527.
11. Maland, pp. 206, 213.

CHAPTER TEN
1. Robinson, p. 530.
2. Ibid., p. 539.
3. Ibid.
4. Charles Chaplin, p. 490.
5. Robinson, p. 546.
6. Ibid., p. 545.
7. Ibid., p. 547.
8. Maland, p. 252.
9. Charles Chaplin, p. 494.
10. Charles Chaplin, Jr., pp. 274–75.
11. Claire Bloom, *Limelight and After: The Education of an Actress* (New York: Harper & Row, 1982), p. 88.
12. Robinson, p. 573, and Maland, p. 281.
13. Maland, p. 301.

CHAPTER ELEVEN
1. McCabe, p. 221.
2. Robinson, p. 574.
3. Maland, p. 319. The magazine in question was the *Saturday Evening Post.*
4. Ibid., p. 324. *A King in New York* was not released in the United States until the mid-1970s.
5. Buster Keaton with Charles Samuels, *My Wonderful World of Slapstick* (Garden City, N.Y.: Doubleday, 1960), p. 270.
6. Ibid., p. 270.
7. Robinson, pp. 599, 755.
8. *Newsweek* 64 (July 27, 1964), p. 78. Quoted in Maland, p. 331.
9. *New York Times*, April 11, 1972, p. 34. Accounts of Chaplin's acceptance speech vary considerably.
10. McCabe, p. 137.

11. William Bayer, *The Great Movies* (New York: Grosset & Dunlap, 1973), p. 67.
12. Kevin Brownlow and John Kobal, *Hollywood: The Pioneers* (New York: Knopf, 1979), p. 142.

FOR FURTHER READING

Brownlow, Kevin, and John Kobal. *Hollywood: The Pioneers.* New York: Knopf, 1979.

Chaplin, Charles. *My Autobiography.* New York: Simon and Schuster, 1964.

My Life in Pictures. New York: Grosset & Dunlap, 1976.

Chaplin, Charles, Jr., with N. and M. Rau. *My Father, Charlie Chaplin.* New York: Random House, 1960.

Chaplin, Lita Grey, with Morton Cooper. *My Life with Chaplin.* New York: Bernard Geis Associates, 1966.

Dardis, Tom. *Keaton: The Man Who Wouldn't Lie Down.* New York: Scribner's, 1979.

Franklin, Joe. *Classics of the Silent Screen.* New York: Citadel Press, 1959.

Huff, Theodore. *Charlie Chaplin.* New York: Henry Schuman, 1951.

Keaton, Buster, with Charles Samuels. *My Wonderful World of Slapstick.* Garden City, NY: Doubleday, 1960.

Kerr, Walter. *The Silent Clowns.* New York: Knopf, 1975.

McCabe, John. *Charlie Chaplin.* Garden City, N.Y.: Doubleday, 1978.

Maland, Charles J. *Chaplin and American Culture: The Evolution of a Star Image.* Princeton, New Jersey: Princeton University Press, 1989.

Manvell, Roger. *Chaplin.* Boston: Little, Brown, 1974.

Robinson, David. *Chaplin: His Life and Art.* New York: McGraw-Hill, 1985.

Sennett, Mack, with Cameron Shipp. *King of Comedy.* Garden City, N.Y.: Doubleday, 1954; San Francisco: Mercury House, 1990.

Tyler, Parker. *Chaplin: Last of the Clowns.* New York: Vanguard Press, 1947. Reprint: New York: Horizon Press, 1972.

INDEX

ABOUT THE AUTHOR

Alan Schroeder is the author of many books for young readers. Two of his titles, *Ragtime Tumpie* and *Carolina Shout!*, have been named ALA Notable Books; in addition, *Tumpie* was a Parents' Choice Award winner and a *Booklist* Children's Editors' Choice. Mr. Schroeder has also written several biographies, including *Booker T. Washington* and *Josephine Baker*. The latter title was chosen by the New York Public Library as a Best Book for the Teen Age. A silent-film enthusiast, Mr. Schroeder lives in Alameda, California.